JUST TO PONDER
NOT TO PREACH

MAVE MOYER

Foreword by Russ Moyer

Published by:
Old Paths Tract Society

ISBN 978-0-9738172-6-3

Printed in the United States of America
For Worldwide Distribution

Eagle Worldwide Enterprises
P.O. Box 39
Copetown, ON, L0R 1J0
Canada

Tel.: (905) 308-9991
Fax.: (905) 308-7798
E-mail: office@eagleworldwide.com
www.EagleWorldwide.com

Cover design by Linda Cove

Dedication

This book of ponderings is dedicated to my wonderful husband
Russ, who is always a source of strength and stability and who has
always shown me love and humility . . .

The special day that you were born
Filled many hearts with pleasure . . .
There's nothing like a son
No other earthly treasure

"He knit you together"
With a purpose and a plan . . .
And committed to watching over you . . .
As you became a man . . .

Father God . . . celebrated at your birth
The good work He had done
By giving to the earth below
One of His favourite sons . . .

He watched you grow and prosper
He saw you at your worst and at your best
He saw you overcome and walk forward
"Called of God "and blessed" . . .

Today . . . He sees the lives you touch . . .
And hears the words of life you share
He sees all those who benefit
Because you truly love and care . . .

He sees your heart so faithful
He sees your life . . . steadfast and true
And He knows how much you love Him
By the obedience He sees in you . . .

He made you an example
To many a guiding light
You have always been willing
To do what's moral and right . . .

Even when others have given up
Or turned their back on you . . .
You have walked in love
And let God's Spirit shine through . . .

You have always shown me
That the "high road" is the best
That only when we "live the Word"
Will we prosper and be blessed . . .

And when others laugh or mock
And speak words of unbelief
We can call on Jesus
He's our comfort and relief . . .

You're a man of true character
Integrity and strength . . .
That I would follow anywhere
No matter the road or its length . . .

The gift of being your wife
Fills me with gratitude and emotion . . .
My gift to you is all my love . . .
And unshakable devotion . . .

Next to Jesus . . . you are the greatest man I know!!!

Table of Contents

Foreword

You are in for a treat . . . no, a Spiritual Word Feast.

I'm honoured that Mave would have me share a foreword for "Just To Ponder Not To Preach." I still remember in the fall of 2000 the first time I heard her deliver one of the poems The Lord gives her. My heart leapt and my spirit saluted. I knew immediately it was indeed the word of The Lord for me, for now, for the body of Christ; that sweet, powerful sound of Glory. Since then, I've heard it again and again; whether it's in an exhortation or an encouraging or comforting word in season for a weary individual, for a church group or for a nation, the sound of Glory rings true.

When she first shared it with me, she thought it was inspired, I knew it was indeed the Word of The Lord. I had the privilege of sitting and serving under one of the great prophetic voices of our generation, Ruth Ward Heflin, at Calvary Pentecostal Campground in Ashland, Virginia and I recognized the beauty of that voice. Whether in a song, hymn or spiritual psalm, whether in prose, in song, in scripture, or in poem, it may be a different administration, a different operation, but the same gift, the same Spirit, and the same Lord. With all the familiarities you will still hear and experience the uniqueness of the anointing of The Holy Spirit through His lovely chosen vessel.

I feel certain you have in your hands a tool, a weapon, a gift from The Lord that will change and transform your life. Whether you choose to read it, use it as a study or a daily devotional, this is a power-packed book of impact. Apply the principals, press into the wisdom and let it transform your love walk.

Dr. Russ Moyer
Eagle Worldwide Ministries
www.EagleWorldwide.com

Introduction

There's nothing more refreshing or rewarding for me than spending some time with The Lord. Time spent in His word pondering and processing is the most valuable time we could ever spend. In the busyness of our world today we may never "have the time" but we have to "take the time" and "make the time" for Him. He has so much to say to us, so much to share with us, so much He wants to pour into us and take out of us. He wants us to become like Him.

Sometimes we just need to lay aside
The busyness of our day . . .
And "make a little time" to spend with Him . . .
And learn of all his ways . . .
We can "live on" His supply . . .
And then . . . "from the overflow" . . .
We can minister to others . . .
And help them rise and grow . . .

Delight yourself in me. THAT is the key, as you come into greater intimacy you'll flow in the "river called ME" . . . come like a child and just believe . . . and from the treasures of heaven you shall receive.

We may never "find" time in our hectic schedule and our overflowing day, but we could "make a little time" to hear what Jesus has to say. You see, that's "our choice" . . . what we will or will not do . . . but I know Jesus wants to spend some time . . . with me and you.

When we make time for Jesus and we let Him have "first place" . . . it's amazing how the rest of the day will seem to pick up pace . . . He'll extend the hours and we'll get all things done . . . when we're faithful to spend some time basking in the "Son."

Try it out my dear friends . . . take some time and see . . . you will hear your Father say . . . Wow . . . you look just like Me.

CHAPTER 1

If You Are Willing And Obedient

If you are willing and obedient . . . you "shall eat" the good of the land. (Isaiah 1:19)

Obedience is the acceptance and living out of the authority and will of God in our lives. It includes submitting to Him and then expressing that submission in our actions, words and thoughts. Obedience is acting in agreement with God . . . and it puts us into a position of power.

Leaders lead first in "obedience"

If we want to be a leader . . . and we want great things to happen in our life so we can actually make a difference in the world we live in . . . we must be willing to spend the time we need to in preparation . . . not just learning what we need to learn . . . but preparing ourselves emotionally for the challenges that lie ahead.

Leadership isn't easy . . . it's rewarding . . . and satisfying but requires hard work . . . lots of which no one ever appreciates or even sees.

Leaders lead in "waiting"

There's a "waiting room" where our dreams are incubated between the time of inception . . . conception . . . and realization. God allows this period of waiting to see if we will stoke the fire of our dream . . . when we don't "see" what we want to see . . . when we want to see it or if we will just lose heart in the midst of the waiting period and allow the spark to cool down and die out.

Most of us don't like to wait. We hate traffic jams . . . checkout lines . . . and delays. We want what we want . . . and we want it "right now."

Spiritually speaking, however, we learn some of life's greatest lessons through the delays and detours of following the leading of Holy Spirit.

The Lord promises to reward us when we submit to His timing. So often when it seems like nothing is happening, "everything" is happening behind the scenes . . . we just can't see it yet.

Leaders lead in "faith"

Waiting is not the accompaniment to faith. Waiting is the DNA of faith . . .

If we will view our time in the "waiting room" as a season of growth and development for our faith . . . we will be that much more ready for the walking out of the manifestation of the dream.

Faith filled waiting on God is never wasting our time . . . In this season, in the natural, we should be spending our time and using our gifts to further the work and service of God in the place He has called us to. Waiting on someone is an action and requires service and serving. Faith without action is dead faith . . .

Most times while we are waiting, God asks us to do things we don't want to do or we don't feel called to do . . . and at those times He's "testing" me and you . . .

Maybe He wants us to work with youth or help with kids' church . . . or be a part of the hospitality team . . . Maybe he wants us to serve the pastor or be an usher. Whatever it is . . . He wants us to be doing something while were waiting on a "bigger something" . . .

If we're willing and obedient during the "time of the test" . . . then when the dream comes to pass we'll be doubly blessed . . . If we hear His voice and follow His command . . . We will eat the "good of the land."

CHAPTER 2

Many are Called, Few are Chosen

2 Chronicles 16:9 . . . For the eyes of The Lord search throughout the earth to strengthen those whose hearts are fully committed to Him.

God is looking to see who will do what they say they will do . . . He is looking for "whosoever" . . . He's looking for us to make the choice . . . God wants people of integrity and character . . . who keep their eyes on Him . . . and who are fully committed to Him.

God anoints those who say yes . . . those who surrender . . . those who give themselves over to His purposes and plans . . . God anoints man . . . The anointing is given without repentance and does not "condone the character of the man or woman of God."

Our character is forged in the yielding of our lives to the Holy Spirit and in allowing Him to have rule and reign. He is our saviour . . . the gift of God . . . and our gift to Him is in making Him Lord.

We must allow God to break us . . . to take us to the end of ourselves . . . and bring us to the beginning of total obedience.

John 12:24 . . . the seed must die to bring forth much fruit . . . We must be willing to die to ourselves if the life of Christ is going to be manifest in us and through us. We must let go of our "old self" and embrace the new life God has purposed in us . . . full of His passion and compassion . . . taking hold of His purpose and His cause for this generation and those to come . . .

Not long ago someone asked for my advice regarding a spiritual struggle. Very simply, this person acts like a Christian on Sunday and like something else the rest of the week.

I do not know all the details . . . and details don't really matter . . . but the frustration of living a double life was obvious. He complained how lonely he was how; he was struggling in his life. He complained bitterly about things that were not based in truth but in wrong perspectives from hurts not effectively dealt with. I told him that he didn't get where he was overnight and he wouldn't get out of this place overnight. I shared that gratitude was a necessary and important trait to have in our lives that it needed to be exercised daily. I exhorted him that we could not allow ourselves to entertain the lies of the enemy . . . that the devil was always working overtime to "dis-appoint" us from our appointment in God.

We must begin every day by choosing to serve the Lord . . . with our thoughts . . . our words . . . and our deeds . . . and then we must follow up that decision with many little right choices moving us in the right direction. That's really what serving the Lord is all about . . . making a decision to do it and then following it up with faith filled action. We can never "straddle the fence." We must choose to serve . . . choose passion . . . choose to be chosen . . .

Many today are living without passion . . . and they have no cause . . .

How can we be filled with HIS spirit and not be filled with passion . . . with His purposes and His plan for today . . . and tomorrow.

He is looking for our heart to be fully His . . . fully yielded . . . fully surrendered.

When we totally let go and let God . . . our lives become one in Him and we can move by the power of His Spirit . . . being led by His love and grace becoming a reflection in the earth of heaven's face . . .

We are called to be those who speak the truth . . . stand for the truth . . . live and die for the truth!! We choose to be "whosoever."

Many "are called" but few "are chosen."

CHAPTER 3

Kingdom Mindset

While I was getting my nails done . . . I over heard a young girl telling her mom how offended she was with her teacher at the end of school. As I listened I thought about how crazy it is the way we perceive things sometimes and how difficult it is for us to receive correction or even direction from people in authority.

As I listened, I thought that what happened was really no big deal and if she could see . . . the teacher's point . . . she could grow through the experience and move forward. Instead, she was stuck in her bad attitude and she was saying very accusatory things about her teacher . . . Her mom kept trying to point out good things about him but she wasn't having any of that.

As I pondered this, a thought came to my heart . . . "Jesus should affect the way we as Christians perceive things."

We have the love of God on the inside. The Bible says that the Holy Spirit himself sealed us with this love. We have this amazing power . . . HIS love shed abroad in our hearts . . . but it does not do us any good if we never pull on that love and access it when our "human" love fails.

Human love is selfish in a way . . . it's the love that loves WHEN you act the right way . . . talk the right way . . . do things the way I want you too, BUT God's love is the supernatural force that empowers us to perceive things through His eyes . . . to love others "in spite of everything" and "because of nothing" This is the way God loves us . . .

"Blessed are the merciful . . . for THEY shall receive mercy" Blessed are the "peace makers" for THEY shall be called the sons of God!

As Christians we should not be this way . . . unsaved people are earthly minded . . . their counsel and wisdom is of the world . . . it is not rooted in the Word of God . . .

This was a lovely young lady who attended the Baptist church and it made me sad to hear her say such hurtful, accusatory things about someone who had poured into her life for a whole year.

We . . . as believers are heirs of the Kingdom of Heaven and we are called to see things through a Kingdom mindset. We are called to live out the issues of our life through the Word of God . . . The entrance of His Word brings light. It brings change. It brings truth.

God is interested in . . . Our relationship with Him . . . Our character as it is developed by the dealings of the Holy Spirit in the working out of our relationship with Him . . . Our relationships with others in the context of our relationship with God.

We are called to be the light to this generation and to those around us in our family, our work place, our church, and we are called of God to not practice the deeds of darkness but rather expose them and walk in the light . . .

Matthew 5:16 says, Let your light shine before men . . . WHY? That they may "SEE" your good deeds and praise your Father in Heaven . . .

Our deeds . . . everything we do . . . and everything we say . . . every thought we have today . . .

Come on my dear friends . . . let us NOT be conformed to this world, but through HIS Word and HIS way let us be truly transformed . . . We have the gift of the Holy Spirit on the inside of us and we CAN do ALL things through Christ . . .

CHAPTER 4

Our Words are Seeds

Do you know that God's Word says that we can have what we say?

In Matthew 8:13 Jesus said, "as you 'believe' so shall it be done unto you." He didn't say, if you believed "right" . . . this is a spiritual principle . . . "AS you believe . . . so shall it be . . . and If you don't believe . . . so it shall not be done . . . Faith . . . "believing" . . . activates the producing of the promise.

God's word always puts a spiritual principle into play . . . whatsoever we "sow" that shall we also "reap" . . . and remember our "words" are "seeds."

It's all about seed time and harvest. Our "words" are "seeds" that produce after like kind. As you plant them . . . you can be assured that a harvest will follow.

Just try speaking something not very nice to your spouse this morning and see for yourself! . . . I assure you . . . A harvest WILL follow . . .

Mark 11:23 tells us that we can have what we say . . . IF we "do not doubt" in our heart . . .

It is so important that we learn how to release faith from our heart when we are exercising our faith to believe . . . We appropriate salvation like this . . . We "confess" with our mouth that Jesus is Lord . . . AND we "believe" in our heart that God raised Him from the dead . . . THEN we are saved . . . first we speak . . . and then we exercise the action of "believing."

We can have what we say . . . but if we listen to the words people are speaking around us today . . . they're saying "what they have."

They are not . . . "calling forth those things that be not as though they were," they are not seeing and decreeing . . . and speaking things into being . . . in the positive! They are "looking at their present situation" and they are speaking what they "see," instead of looking through the eyes of faith and seeing and decreeing what God says is true . . . what God says is possible.

There has been a generation that has allowed the enemy access to their words and they have spoken negative and hurtful things over their children . . . their employer . . . their spouse their own life . . . and have reaped a harvest according to the seeds they have planted with their own words . . .

We have become so programmed by the natural world we live in, that we have been seduced into speaking for the wrong side . . . and have even spoken the devils language . . .

Some of us still need to be praying for crop failure . . . on things we have said!

We are made in the likeness and image of God . . . He SPOKE his world into being . . . and so do we speak our world into being . . .

The Bible clearly instructs us to "teach our mouth to speak right things" and to "order our conversation rightly."

As believers . . . we are called to follow the example Jesus gave us . . . He didn't say anything that he didn't hear the Father say . . .

WOW . . . I know that's a hard act to follow . . . but if we would just be purposeful with our words and weigh them "before" we say them . . . what a difference it would make in the things we say . . .

The Word tells us to be like dear children . . . imitating our Father . . . walking, talking and doing like He does . . .

We can make all the "excuses" we want . . . excuses only give us opportunity to fail . . .

We can start all the "arguments" we want . . . but in the light of His truth an argument pales . . . the "truth" of His Word will always BE . . . He has given His Word to you and me . . . that we might have life abundant "every day" . . . in the things "we do" and the things "we say" . . . Let's take God at HIS WORD . . . He is NOT a man that He should lie . . .

God's Word in our mouth is as powerful as God's Word in his mouth . . . it's not about "the mouth" BUT "The Word." His Word . . . conceived in "our heart" formed by "our words" and "spoken" brings His creative power to bear on the situations of our lives . . .

Doubt sees the obstacles . . . and faith sees the way . . . doubt sees the darkness and faith . . . sees the day . . . doubt dares to take a step . . . and faith soars on high . . . doubt questions . . . who believes?? And FAITH answers . . . 1 . . . 1 believe!!!!

1 believe Lord . . . 1 see and decree and 1 receive . . . according to your Word and plan . . . 1 take hold of my promised land!

CHAPTER 5

Letting go of fear

Fear lurks in the silent darkness, unwanted—hated. Its power is so great that even when ignored or denied it can still control our destiny.

If we do the things we fear then the death of fear is certain . . . but most of the time fear keeps us from stepping in and stepping up . . . and we refuse to face our fears . . .

Fear has an enormous capacity to influence our behaviour and the outcome of the circumstances we are faced with . . . "fear" sees the obstacle . . . and "faith" sees the way . . . "Fear" sees the darkness and "faith" sees the day! "Fear" dreads to take a step while "faith" soars on high . . . fear questions . . . who believes and faith answers . . . I believe!!

I challenge you today . . . COME OUT of fear . . . and unbelief. Let go of negative attitudes that try to hold you in bondage. Say NO to the pessimism that is all around you . . . and see the possibilities in God for your life today!!

The enormous potential in your life can only be unlocked by YOU . . .

The impossible becomes possible when we let go of fear and move into the realm of faith . . .

Our "act of faith" triggers the release of God's miracle power . . .

Just be obedient . . . whatever He tells you to do . . . just do it!!!

John 2:5 Turning water into wine seemed impossible that day . . . but faith and obedience go a long way . . . We can't let our senses rule our life . . . we walk by faith not by sight . . .

Mark 9:13 IF you CAN BELIEVE . . . ALL things "are possible" to him WHO BELIEVES!!!!

Let's be those who believe . . . and receive . . . let's be those who help others to see and achieve . . . let's walk in the wonder working power of His grace . . . always reflecting heaven's face!

He is the God of "endless" possibilities!

CHAPTER 6

Arise and shine

Isaiah 60:1-2 "Arise, shine, for your light has come . . . and the glory of the Lord rises upon you. See . . . darkness covers the earth . . . and thick darkness is over the peoples . . . but the Lord rises upon you . . . and HIS glory appears over you."

This scripture does not say . . . that darkness covers the "unbelieving" people. We are all subject to being deceived if we do not listen to . . . learn and "live" in the Word of God . . . The Bible says that the entrance of HIS WORD brings light and that we are called to be "DOERS" of the Word not "hearers" only . . . deceiving ourselves . . .

Amazing how many seasoned and long time Christians still "fight" against applying the Word of God . . . and choose to live in the flesh instead of in the Spirit . . . Many would rather be offended . . . play the blame game and operate outside the principles of God then make their "flesh" line up with the truth of God's Word.

Today more than ever we are seeing the separation in the church between those who are following God through His Word and those who are confessing with their lips while the "active" part of their faith and lives are still manifesting self . . . and old patterns and behaviours that they "refuse" to let go of . . .

The ONLY thing that will "change us" is the "decision and follow through" of allowing God's Word to have first place in our lives . . . first place over our "feelings" . . . our "emotions" . . . our "desires" . . . our "pride" . . .

God's Word and His way are truth . . . anything other than this for a Christian is wrong . . . and will never bring change but will allow us to go around the mountain again and again . . .

God's Word is unlike any other word. It is alive. Jesus said, "The words that I have spoken to you are spirit and they are life" . . . John 6:63

When God speaks . . . things change! When we "will apply" the Word to the situations and circumstances of our every day life we will have good success.

Everything around us . . . all of creation . . . exists because "God said it." He spoke it all into existence . . . and we speak our own world into existence everyday . . . by the words we say . . . Good or bad . . . happy or sad . . . we are responsible for the words of our own mouth . . . and for the action we decide to take . . .

Proverbs 1:31 says . . . they will eat the fruit of their own words and ways and be filled with the fruit of their schemes.

But "His Word" and "ways" active in our life will create good circumstances and change situations that are wrong . . .

God's Word brings life . . . it creates faith . . . produces change . . . rebukes the devil . . . causes miracles to happen . . . heals disease . . . eases hurts and pains . . . and can cure our financial ills . . .

His Word . . . builds integrity and character . . . transforms circumstances . . . overcomes adversity . . . brings joy unspeakable . . . defeats temptation in our lives . . . gives us hope . . . releases God's power . . . transforms our minds . . . calls things into being and guarantees our future will not only be successful and prosperous but that we will live forever because we have believed His Word!!

We cannot live without the Word of God! We should never take it for granted . . . by not applying it to our life every day . . . There is really no excuse for a believer to operate outside His Word . . . and if we do . . . we will have ongoing troubles and problems and concerns . . . His Word is the remedy for all those "earthly" ills.

A Christian who "says" they know the Word and will not live by its principles and truth . . . is like a man who knows how to swim yet chooses to drown . . .

His Word is as essential to our life as food . . . water and oxygen . . . "Sanctify them by the truth . . . your Word is truth." John 17:17

CHAPTER 7

Live Out of the Overflow

I saw the whirlwind of the world and busyness and the chaotic motion of the wind . . . then I heard a hush . . . and felt the wind of the Spirit come in . . . I saw a different kind of whirlwind in the place of ease . . . and I saw the breeze softly blowing the leaves of the trees . . . I smelt a sweet fragrance in the cool of the day and I heard the voice of God softly call out and say . . .

Come away beloved . . . into a deeper place . . . where I can mould and make you in the furnace of My grace . . . a place of love and acceptance . . . a place of intimacy . . . where you can know me more and I will make you more like me . . .

Sometimes we just need to lay aside
The busyness of our day
and "make a little time" to spend with Him . . .
and learn of all his ways . . .
we can "live on" His supply . . .
and then . . . "from the overflow" . . .
we can minister to others
and help them rise and grow . . .

Delight yourself in me . . . THAT is the key . . . as you come into greater intimacy you'll flow in the "river called ME" . . . come like a child and just believe . . . and from the treasures of heaven you shall receive . . .

We may never "find" time in our hectic schedule
and our over-worked day . . .
but we could "make a little time" to hear
what Jesus has to say . . . ?

You see that's "our choice"
what we will or will not do . . .

but I know Jesus wants to spend some time . . .
with me and you . . .

When we make time for Jesus and we let Him have "first place" . . .
it's amazing how the rest of the day will seem to pick up pace . . .
He'll extend the hours and we'll get all things done . . .
when we're faithful to spend some time basking in the "son"

Try it out my dear friends . . . take some time and see . . . you will hear your Father
say . . . Wow . . . you look just like me . . .

CHAPTER 8

Times and Seasons

Can you hear the sound of the bee keeper . . . ?

He is calling to his people right now . . . He is recruiting and calling His people to a place of true accountability and responsibility . . . it's time to rise up and "be the church."

So many churches today have become a bless me club . . . a social outing . . . a place where there is no power to bring real change and fruit that lasts . . . the gospel being preached is enticing words of men but it lacks the demonstrations of the Spirit of God!

The fullness of time is upon us . . . the "beginning of sorrows" has begun . . . and it won't be long before we see the Son . . .

The days of darkness are upon us . . . and gross darkness covers the people. Sooner or later we have to rise up and do something with the gifts God has given us . . . He gave supernatural gifts that we might minister to one another in the manifold grace of God . . .

Most of the time the church is busy arguing over "are the gifts for today" or have they passed away?

Many traditional churches spread "their teaching" that the five fold ministry has passed away . . . that there are no apostles and the prophets for today . . . that they are finished . . . and that ministry is through . . . yet the Bible says the last thing Jesus did was give them to me and you . . .

"They" say . . . miracles no longer happen and we no longer need to set the captives free . . . they say there is no more deliverance and healing . . . can that really be??

We've become so good at negating the Word of God . . .
And deciding what "we believe" is still true . . .
That we've presented a powerless gospel
Even if we never meant to . . .

God is looking for a people
Who will stand right up and say . . .
We believe in resurrection power
And that it still exists today . . .

He's the same yesterday, today, forever . . . His ways will always be . . . He's poured
out His Spirit and He works through you and me . . . SO let's co-labour with the Lord
and do what he's called us to . . . we're not waiting on Him . . . He's waiting on me
and you!

CHAPTER 9

God kind of Faith

Man is a spirit being. Do you believe that we . . . being made in the likeness of God are capable of operating in the same measure of faith as God?? He said he has given to all men a "measure of faith" . . . NOT a half measure . . . but a FULL measure.

In Mark 9:23, Jesus said, IF you CAN BELIEVE, ALL things are possible . . . to him THAT BELIEVES . . . this is good news . . . if we can believe and NOT DOUBT in our hearts . . . we can say to whatever issue . . . whatever sickness . . . whatever mountain . . . be removed and be cast into the sea . . . we can be assured that whatever we say will come to pass and we will have whatever we say . . . PRAISE GOD our words are containers of "power"!

This is a spiritual law . . . God never does anything without saying it first. He releases His faith through His words . . . God's words in our mouth are as powerful as His Word in His mouth . . .

Ephesians 5:1 says, be imitators of God as children imitate their parents. Walk like Him . . . Talk like Him . . . act like Him. Jesus came as the exact expression of His Father . . . He spoke to the wind and sea . . . He spoke to the demons . . . and to the fig tree . . . Jesus released His faith through His Words . . . He didn't say anything He didn't hear his Father say . . . Words are the most powerful things in the universe!!!! O God please help us to have such a revelation of this truth that our conversation would be totally transformed.

I know that if Jesus came to me today and said "from now on everything you say will come to pass" . . . I would certainly be mindful of my words and would begin to order my conversation rightly . . . knowing that I will have what I say . . .

Well, the Word of God is true . . . that's just like Jesus speaking to me and you . . . His Word promises us today . . . that we will have what we believe and say . . .

Our words carry faith or fear . . . the treasure of our heart is made manifest by the words we speak . . . our words speak the solution or the problem . . . our words program our heart for victory or defeat . . . the creative power in the word is produced by the belief in the heart . . . then as we speak what the heart believes we set in motion the faith that receives. The "seed" of the Word . . . produces after "like kind."

We MUST learn to release faith from the heart through our words . . . Jesus said in Matthew 8:13, as you have believed, so shall it be done unto you . . .

This is seed time and harvest . . . the words we speak will produce after like kind.

A harvest of our words will follow those things we say . . . let's teach our mouth to speak right things today . . .

Let the "words" of my mouth . . . AND the "meditations" of my heart . . . be acceptable in your sight . . . O Lord!!!!

CHAPTER 10

Building Relationship with the Holy Spirit

It's time to "build relationship" with the Holy Spirit . . . a relationship is the way in which two or more people . . . objects . . . or concepts are connected . . . the state of being connected. We need a Holy Ghost connection . . .

Jesus told the disciples it was better for them if He left . . . so that the Holy Spirit might come and be within them . . . and it's the same for us today . . .

We are called to walk in the "Present Day Ministry" of Jesus . . . He has not changed . . . He is still the same . . . yesterday . . . today and forever . . . the works that Jesus did . . . were accomplished by the power of the "Holy Spirit" . . . and so are the works we will do . . . "IF" we will "do" them . . . but so many today are busy telling us why we can't . . . or trying to discredit those who are . . . or exercising skepticism and doubt instead of looking through the eyes of faith and believing God!

Some who are sick . . . would rather believe God is "teaching them something" by making them sick . . . instead of believing that He already took all of their illness and disease . . . and that he would not make us sick . . . anymore than we would make our own children sick!!!

Jesus exercised His faith in His Father and called upon the administrative power of the Holy Spirit to bring forth the miracle.

In the beginning . . . the earth was without form and void . . . and darkness was on the face of the deep . . . and the "Spirit" of God was hovering over the face of the waters. Then God said, "Let there be light"; and there was light . . . and by the power of the "spoken word" and the releasing of the "administrative and creative power" the Holy Spirit brought forth that which was spoken . . .

33

Here we see Jesus . . . (the Word) God (the Father) . . . and the Holy Spirit . . . all three . . . the trinity . . . working together that the miracle might come to be!!!

Can we learn to walk and talk and flow with Him . . . All of creation is awaiting the manifestations of the sons of God . . . those who are "led by the Spirit of God"

Not by logic . . . or feelings . . . or emotions . . . not by head knowledge . . . or earthly understanding . . . but by relationship and revelation . . . and by believing His Word is full of enough power to bring itself to pass and calling forth those things that be not as though they were . . . accepting the truth that we will have what we say . . . and exercising it by seeing and decreeing for God . . . and moving in the Spirit to see the manifestation of that which we seeing and believing for . . .

In Him we can do ALL things . . .

Only believe . . . Only believe
All things are possible
Only believe!!

CHAPTER 11

Child-like Faith

Unless we become like children . . . humble . . . teachable and trusting . . . we will never grow into the spiritual people God intends for us to be . . .

Jesus gives us a child like faith . . . He wants us to have a child like faith.

The very heart of the Gospel is a mandate for child-like faith . . . The bottom line to salvation is being able to say three words: I NEED JESUS!

The only thing standing between man and God is pride . . . Humbling ourselves, admitting, believing, confessing . . . It's all about Jesus . . . When we stand before our God we never want to hear: depart from me for I never KNEW you!

That word . . . "KNEW" we should underline and highlight.
It's a "KNOWING" . . . a relationship . . . NOT RELIGION!

Some people are far to "full of self" to have child like faith . . . child like faith takes a willingness to believe God "no matter what" . . . and to "act" on that which they "say" they believe . . . Our faith is first evidenced by our words . . . and then by our actions . . . Faith without works is dead . . . lifeless alone . . .

As we "prophetically" walked and took ground for God in the service tonight . . . it was an act of our obedience and faith . . . a physical response to His Word . . . and His direction . . . to "Rise Up" and take ground for His Kingdom . . .

As we respond in love with "child like" faith to the bidding of God we will see great things in the season ahead . . . His Word says if you love me . . . you'll obey me . . . and obedience is better than sacrifice . . .

Sometimes ... He might ask us to do something we don't want to do ... or something we don't understand ... something that we feel silly doing ... like ... what's the point? but if we will do it "by faith" ... we will see the fulfillment of what we are believing him for ... There is no substitute for "child like faith."

Knowledge puffs up ... and love builds up ... When we "obey" we evidence our love ... and our trust in Him ...

Today more than ever we need more of God ... more "revelation" and less information ... Less "facts" and more "truth" ... facts ... they change ... and man's knowledge ... fades away ... but the Word of God will always REMAIN!

Many may argue this but I always say ... you can argue with my "opinion" but not with the experience I had in God today!!! ... Religion doesn't get experience ... but you can't have relationship without experiences ...

Without faith it is impossible to please Him ... for he that comes to God must believe that He "IS" and that He is a rewarder of them that diligently seek him.

CHAPTER 12

Setting a Godly Example

We do a great injustice to our children ... when we take the "place of God" in their lives ... only Jesus can solve their problems ... provide for their needs ... deal with their issues and make a way ... for them to become who they are "supposed to be." He is their provider ... their Saviour ... their ultimate judge ...

We do a further injustice when we do not direct them to the Word of God ... where they can chart a successful course for their lives ... His Word answers all things and reproves us in all things ... His Word is life and truth and as believers we must always encourage them to be "doers" of the Word ...

It is only in the "doing" that the Word works in our lives ... Faith "without corresponding works ... is dead ... lifeless ..."

We will all "stand alone" at the judgment seat of Christ and we will all answer individually for our own behaviour ... words ... and deeds ...

Ultimately the responsibility and consequences of our children's choices are between them and God ... God has given them and all of us a "free will." They are free to choose for themselves what they will and will not do ... but they are never free from the consequences of their choice ...

"Our choice" as parents should always be to direct them to Him and His ways ... to His Word and the standard He has set for them and us. His Word is a blueprint for success ... when we are doers of His Word. His Word cannot return void ... it WILL accomplish whatever it is sent to do. His Word has supernatural power to produce ...

We are called to be the example in our children's lives . . . They may "not choose" to "follow our example" . . . but we must BE that example anyway . . . in everything we "say" and "DO" . . . let our children "SEE" Jesus in me and you!!

Thanking God for He is the Father of ALL of us . . . who believe!!!

CHAPTER 13

Honouring Our Parents

God exhorts us to honour our father and mother. He values honouring parents enough to include it in the Ten Commandments (Exodus 20:12) and again in the New Testament.

"Children . . . obey your parents in the Lord, for this is right. Honour your father and mother which is the first commandment with a promise, so that it may be well with you, and that you may live long on the earth" . . . Honouring parents is the only command in Scripture that promises long life as a reward. Those who honour their parents are blessed. In contrast, those with a "depraved mind" and those who exhibit ungodliness in the last days are characterized by disobedience to parents (Romans 1:30; 2 Timothy 3:2).

Solomon, the wisest man, urged us to respect our parents. Proverbs 1:8; 13:1; 30:17.

Although we may no longer be directly under their authority, we cannot outgrow God's command to honour our parents. Even Jesus, God the Son, submitted Himself to both His earthly parents . . . Luke 2:51 . . . and His heavenly Father . . . Matthew 26:39.

Following Jesus' example, we should treat our parents the way we would reverentially approach our heavenly Father . . . Hebrews 12:9; Malachi 1:8

Exodus 20:12—Honour thy father and thy mother: that thy days may be long upon the land which the LORD thy God giveth thee.

Proverbs 20:20—Who ever curses his father or his mother . . . his lamp shall be put out in obscure darkness.

Ephesians 6:2-3—Honour thy father and mother . . . which is the first commandment with promise

1 Peter 5:5-6—Likewise, ye younger, submit yourselves unto the elder. Yea, all [of you] be subject one to another, and be clothed with humility: for God resists the proud, and gives grace to the humble.

Deuteronomy 21:18-21—If a man have a "stubborn and rebellious son" . . . which will not obey the voice of his father, or the voice of his mother, and [that], when they have chastened him, dishonours and will not hearken unto them . . .

1 Timothy 5:1—Rebuke not an elder, but intreat him as a father . . . and the younger men as brethren.

Proverbs 1:8-9—Hear, my son, your father's instruction, and forsake not your mother's teaching, for they are a graceful garland for your head and pendants for your neck.

Thank God for Godly Fathers . . . grandfathers and Spiritual Fathers . . . We give honour to those who honour is due . . .

CHAPTER 14

Your Life is Like a Light House

This morning when 1 was sharing my time with The Lord 1 began to realize how important it is in these days where darkness is covering the earth . . . and "gross darkness" the people . . . that 1 let the light of His love . . . and grace . . . and truth shine through me . . . That He has called me to be a light for others to see . . . That the privilege of salvation . . . comes with responsibility . . . We did not get saved just for our sake . . . but also for the sake of many others . . .

God has made us a light house and has a right and true expectation of me and you . . . that we would shine with that light . . . letting it affect others too . . .

Let your "life" house be a light house
As you Stand strong in me . . .
Be Led by my Spirit
And allow your faith to see . . .

I'm your refuge and your fortress
In me . . . you can fully trust
To walk in my covenant promise
Faith in me is a must . . .

Faith that stands believing
No matter how it seems . . .
Faith that endures the trials
And keeps its eyes upon the dream . . .

Faith that through the pain . . .
Knows joy will spring forth in that place . . .
As you are processed and refined
In the furnace of my grace . . .

Shine your light for others
That they may look and see
That the beauty that's inside you
Is because you carry me . . .

As you let your "life" house be my light house
And you move in all my ways . . .
You will change the lives of others
And make a difference every day . . .

For the time in short . . . the time is NOW
To arise . . . step fully in
Shine your light so others . . .
Can follow me and win . . .

Day by day . . . the clock is ticking . . .
And many lives are cast away . . .
Arise and shine . . . your light as come . . .
We're in the final days . . .

And as the darkness covers
The earth and people too
We must make the decision
It's up to me and you . . .

Will we arise and do our part
And shine with the light of His grace
Or will the Spirit pass us by
As another takes our place . . .

We are called and appointed
To walk fully in His plan
But the choice is really up to us
He's given free will to every man ...

We can make a difference
When our "life" becomes His light
And we can shine and show the way
For others to win the fight ...

Or we can hide it under a bushel
Or a burden or a care ...
Not really believing Him ourselves
Not trusting that He's there ...

Our light will be diminished
If we let "little things" get in our way
If we aren't mindful of the things we do
And of the things we say

So let's decide ... to rise to the occasion
We are God's Light house and design
But we can't be a beacon
If our light don't shine!!!

The Lord spoke to me and said the moon has no light of its own ... it shines with the light of the sun ... and YOU are like the moon for you have no light of your own ... but you shine with the "light of the son."

When the things of the earth pass between the sun and the moon there will be an eclipse . . . and the moon will cease to shine . . . and when we allow the things of this earth to come between us and the son . . . our duties . . . distractions . . . divisions . . . discord and even our delights . . . then we will cease to shine . . . and we will have an eclipse of our heart . . .

Let's be mindful to not let the things of the earth come in between us and God . . . so we may continue to shine forth with the light of His mercy . . . grace and love . . .

That our heart will stay soft and pliable and our love will not wax cold . . .

Our "life house" yielded to the "son" will become a "light house" and a sign . . .

But we can't be a beacon if our lights don't shine!!!!

CHAPTER 15

Doers and Not Just Hearers

How blessed we are as followers of Jesus . . . to have the Word of God that we might chart our course in life and be a success . . . Those that are not "doers" of the word and "hearers" only . . . are deceived and will not prosper in the ways that God intended.

During our time in Buffalo . . . MANY were healed. It was amazing to see the number of people who had one leg shorter than the other and how their body was out of alignment . . . We all watched in amazement while legs actually grew out and people we're free from leg pain . . . back pain . . . hips out of joint and arthritis . . . One member of the fellowship walked out without his walker declaring he didn't need it any more!! PRAISE GOD!!

The Lord spoke to me and said HIS body is out of alignment too . . . many are in pain and causing pain to other parts of the body because they are not in right alignment . . . they are "out of joint."

When we are "out of joint" we are . . . dis-located . . . not working well together . . . disordered . . . not in proper connection with . . . and because of this the whole body suffers . . .

The Lord clearly showed me that only when we "walk it out" in the WORD will we ever be in right alignment . . . He has structured HIS body to be aligned with HIM . . . for He is the "chief cornerstone" and every living stone (all of us) must line up with him . . . and His Word . . .

If we have an issue . . . a problem . . . or if we are having pain or causing pain . . . we need to get in alignment with the Word of God and do what HE says to do . . . not what our "flesh . . . or feelings" want us to do . . . or what our "pride" wants us to do . . . but what HE wants.

We cause ourselves pain and we cause the whole body to suffer when we will not come into right alignment.

Hear the Word of the Lord . . . That is to "hear it" when it is preached . . . When the Word of God is declared to the body . . . we must as members of that body . . . give our "attention" to the Word . . . How blessed we are when God sends a message through a woman or a man directly to our hearts . . . We have the opportunity to hear from Heaven . . . and we should take full advantage of that opportunity and learn all that we can . . . His Word is sent to heal us . . . reprove us . . . correct us . . .

It isn't enough to just listen to a preacher preach. Scientists tell us that people only retain about 10% of what they hear. We need to allow the continual washing of the water of the word to do the sanctifying work of "renewing" our mind . . . We must live by every word that comes out of the mouth of God.

So many Bible school scholars and graduates have head knowledge of the Word . . . but as soon as the trials of life start and the storms of relationship begin to brew . . . and things are just not going the way they want them to . . . we soon see if the Word is alive in their heart or just stored in their head . . .

If we are "strong in The Lord and in the power of His might" . . . then we can do ALL things through Him who makes us strong!! If we are not strong in His Word . . . through the action of living it out . . . then we are limited by our own natural resources . . . and ability . . .

James 1:22 . . . says, Do not merely "listen to the Word" and so deceive yourselves . . . Do what it says.

Unfortunately . . . the living out and walking out of the Word is often neglected by many Christians . . . even those that are called as leaders in the church today . . . are succumbing to their feelings . . . emotions and self will instead of submitting their will to the Word of God and doing the right thing . . . This will cause the whole body to be out of alignment . . . and to suffer . . . Leaders are called to "lead by example" Leadership is not a "position" it's an action . . .

True leaders will be revealed not by "what they say" but rather by the "action" they take and what they do . . . in line with the Word of God . . .

If we will determine in our heart that we will not just "listen" . . . but we will "learn" and "live" in the Word then . . . we will not be so easily put out of joint by those who choose not to . . . even though they will probably have a hard time with us because we do.

When Joshua became the leader of the people of Israel . . . and before he led them into the promised land, God said to him, "This book of the law shall not depart out of your mouth: but you shall meditate therein day and night, that you may observe "to do" according to "all that is written therein" for THEN you will make your way prosperous, and then you will have good success" . . . The words "good success" are used only once in the whole Bible . . . in this verse.

Joshua's "good success" was dependent upon allowing the principles of God's Word to be the foundation upon which the nation was to built.

Today it is no different . . . God's principles are still just as true, eternal, and valid . . . If the foundation of our life is established on the Word of God we will have "good success."

CHAPTER 16

True Prosperity

This morning the Lord said to me . . . the problem MY people have with prosperity is they think it's about "money only" . . . He said I want them to prosper . . . and be in good health as their soul prospers . . . He is interested in the prosperity of His servants.

The last few nights at camp God has been speaking to us about the importance of sowing the seed . . . not just finances . . . but the seed of our children . . . the seed of our talents and abilities . . . our possessions . . . our time . . . everything we have is a seed . . .

I had a dream where the Lord showed me that His people were holding back . . . not just financially but in many areas of giving . . . not willing to give of their time and talents . . . not willing to take the time to pray and be in the Word. He showed me people who had resources that we're not giving the way they should and I saw them being stopped up . . .

He showed me where he actually caused a "moving out" of some people in areas where they were not being faithful . . . because he had to. Remember . . . He "TAKES DELIGHT" in the prosperity of His people and He will reposition and realign us that we might become obedient to His Word so that we would walk in the blessing . . . the full reward . . . I don't know about you, but I want the full reward!

Prosperity comes when we walk in the truth . . . Deuteronomy 8:18 says, . . . You SHALL remember the Lord your God: for it is HE that has given you the power to GAIN wealth . . . (why) . . . that He "may establish HIS covenant" which he swore unto thy fathers . . . as it is this day . . . God gave us the power to gain wealth that WE would establish His covenant . . . His Word into all the earth . . . that we would make disciples of nations . . . make disciples in the streets in the marketplace in the church . . .

God's very nature is abundance . . . Jesus came that we might have life and life abundantly . . . BUT every promise of God is conditional . . . He wants us to prosper as our soul prospers . . .

I'm telling you that a sinner who possesses wealth has only a temporary reservoir . . . and their "self made, self sufficient" status can be the very thing that keeps them from coming to the knowledge of true riches in Christ!

In my own life I went from rags to riches . . . not being willing to have my kids grow up like I did . . . I sacrificed and worked and made my way to attaining wealth to live the way I wanted to live . . . then I found the true heart of God and everything I had achieved fell apart and fell away . . . leaving me in a place of riches to rags . . . but as I pressed into knowing Him . . . and as I began to give out of my need . . . and as I trusted in His Word and believed that if I would seek Him first ALL things would be added . . . He was faithful to do His part . . . and I went from rags to "His riches in Glory" . . . Hallelujah!!!! . . . His riches that nothing can take away . . . the blessing of the Lord maketh rich and He adds NO SORROW to it . . . Praise God . . . when we are obedient to Him and to His Word . . . when we are obedient to give and trust Him for the increase . . . He is able . . . He will do it . . . He will make it happen . . . He will give . . . He will bless!!!!!! HE TAKES DELIGHT . . . in the prosperity of his children!!!!!!!!

CHAPTER 17

Walking in His Fear

Today more than ever we need to walk in the "fear of The Lord."

A reverence for His Word and a decision to allow His Lordship in our lives. Salvation is a free gift of God . . . It is forgiveness and grace "offered freely" for our sin.

Allowing His Lordship however, is an act of our will . . . a decision and desire to allow God to rule and reign on the throne of our lives. The throne of our lives is not a seat made for two . . . and God will not share it with me and you . . .

Today the church is sadly lacking in the "Fear of The Lord." Many have embraced a "feel good Gospel" and a dangerous hyper grace message that no longer brings conviction . . . correction and consecration.

Believers today are still called to be set apart . . . to answer the call and to walk in the purposes and plans of God . . . not when "we feel like it" but according the Word and the will of God . . .

I heard a young man one day so flippantly say . . . "Isn't it good how Jesus died for all our "future screw ups" . . . and I thought . . . man, you got a screw loose . . . to so disrespectfully discern the Grace of God . . . It may have been "freely given" but He paid a great price for it . . . and we should value and esteem this empowering agent called grace that makes it possible for us to live a life free from sin.

All men sin and fall short of the glory of God . . . If any man says he doesn't sin then he makes God a liar . . . Even when we do fall short . . . saying things we shouldn't . . . entertaining wrong thoughts and behaving in ways that grieve the heart of God . . . He is still faithful to forgive us "WHEN" we "confess and repent" and turn away from the "sin" and He restores us again to righteousness.

The fear of The Lord is the beginning of wisdom
It keeps us free from sin . . .
If we operate in the flesh
Every evil thing will win . . .

If we do not yield our bodies
And submit to God our every deed . . .
We can be taken off track by the enemy
Instead of following the Spirit's lead . . .

When we do not yield our minds . . .
Our thoughts . . . will be our own . . .
And we will meditate on things . . .
That God does not condone . . .

When we do not yield our tongue
It can be set on fire from hell . . .
And instead of speaking God's truth
We'll repeat the lies we hear the devil tell . . .

The fear of the Lord is the beginning of wisdom
In our life . . . it must take first place . . .
Then instead of moving in the flesh
We will function in God's grace . . .

It is always our decision . . .
What we will do . . . or say . . .
We can walk in the blessing of obedience
Or eat the fruit of our own way . . .

God is looking for a people . . .
Who will "DO" . . . and "Hear" . . .
Those walking in "His love"
And walking in "His fear."

CHAPTER 18

Harvesters

There is a harvest set to happen and some of the harvesters are missing in action . . . the "winds of change" are blowing . . . and rather than "allowing" change . . . and "embracing" change some are being "blown out" of the field . . . by the same wind that was sent to "bring change" and increase. Deception and familiar spirits are operating and my people are being distracted from my purposes, divisions . . . discord and dis-appointments are disappointing my people from their appointment in me . . .

Some of my appointed
To this season of reaping . . .
Are missing in action . . .
They are murmuring and weeping . . .

They've left their position
And laid down my plan . . .
They're away without leave
And offended of man . . .

They are not willing . . .
To make wrong things right . . .
So they forfeit the victory
Not being ready to fight . . .

Their love waxes cold
And soon they lose heart
They "fall away" from me
And their life falls apart . . .

"But" the fullness of time . . .
In this season and day . . .
Will bring forth the promise
And open the way . . .

For the reapers to harvest
Where they did not sow
And the crops that they tended
Will continue to GROW

Those that are "faithful"
Will find my reward
Those walking in unity
And in one accord . . .

Those walking in love
By faith . . . they shall see
Those things that I promised . . .
Will all come to be . . .

Don't be "out of position"
Or you cannot win . . .
Don't be at the airport
When your ship comes in . . .

The Lord said to me that many are "falling away" in this day . . . Many are caught up in a self pity-party and are . . . by their wrong actions and attitudes . . . separating themselves from the body . . . and His purposes and plan

He said that they isolate . . . or re-locate . . . they make their decisions based on emotions . . . feelings and offense . . . instead of making their flesh come into alignment with the Word of God and My Spirit . . . and they run from the very situation that I AM using to change them . . .

He said this is the very thing that will keep them from harvesting in the fields where they have sown . . . they have grown weary and are missing out on their "due season."

They are missing in action . . .
Away without leave . . .
They've allowed the enemy
To divide and deceive . . .

It is always the "hottest"
Before the crop is complete . . .
This is true for us also . . .
So . . . God turns up the heat . . .

Until we are refined
And brought forth as gold . . .
Until we are moved by His Spirit
And the Word we've been told . . .

Till we walk in His ways
In His love and His grace
Until we reflect
His life and His face.

He will not be finished
Until his project's complete
So . . . let's get with the program
Before HE turns up the heat.

The harvest is ready
It's white in the field
We are His reapers.
The promise is sealed

Let's not be "dis-appointed"
From our "appointment" today
For this IS our season
He is making a way . . .

So as we "stand" believing
In "our place" . . . and in His plan
We shall receive
From our Father's hand . . .

A bountiful blessing
A harvest . . . plentiful and great
A promise fulfilled . . .
That was well worth the wait . . .

Let us not grow weary in well doing . . . for in "due season" we shall reap a harvest . . .
if we do not lose heart . . . Galatians 6:9

Chapter 19

Avoid Godless Chatter

True justice imperatively demands that we should never condemn another until we have heard what he or she has to say for himself or herself.

The Bible says that . . . One tale is good "until" another be told.

Proverbs 18:8: "The words of a talebearer are as wounds . . . and they go down into the innermost parts of the belly."

Tale bearing and lying destroys . . . In Proverbs . . . the Bible says that God hates a false witness . . . one who pours out lies . . . a person who sows discord . . . a lying tongue.

I'm sure you have been with someone who sits around and "talks" about others . . . telling "their perception" of things and their "side" of the story . . . the Bible says in . . . Proverbs 18:17 . . . Any one's story "sounds true" until another comes and sets the record straight.

We should be careful how we are "talking." The Bible tells us to "teach our mouth" to speak "right things" . . . and that we should "order" our conversation rightly . . . God is the silent visitor at every table . . . the invisible party on every telephone line . . . He is behind every closed door . . . and hears every thought on our heart. There are NO secrets from God who is everywhere and in everything . . . He is always present . . . He never leaves us . . . or forsakes us . . . In everything we say and in everything we do . . . He is "with" me and you . . .

He loves the family of God . . . He doesn't just love me and you . . . He loves ALL the others too . . .

In 2 Timothy he speaks to us and reminds me and you . . .

Remind and warn "my people"
That they should not quarrel over words . . .
That they should be the example
Of "doing" what they've heard . . .

Quarrelling . . . is of NO value
And hurts those that listen and pay heed
YOU be a workman approved
Who correctly handles the "seed."

Avoid godless chatter . . .
Don't indulge and entertain
It hurts those who "listen"
And it spreads like gangrene.

The "only cure" for gangrene . . . is to "cut it off" . . . If we don't . . . He will. He loves the "body" too much to have it affected by this "disease." It is serious and potentially life-threatening to the rest of the body . . . He said to avoid godless chatter . . . because those who indulge in it . . . will become more ungodly . . .

Let's be "honest" in all of our dealings with others. We are in the season of alignment . . . We are going to be called of God more than ever in these days to "practice" what we preach . . . or we will not preach . . .

CHAPTER 20

Seeking God in the Storm

A "natural disaster" is NOT a "supernatural" act of God!

When a tornado or another type of horrific storm ravishes a State or a Province . . . a community . . . a City, it is not God "punishing" the people who live there . . . It is "very predictable" for certain states to experience storms and tornados in "this season" . . . I remember being in Oklahoma during my Bible school years and taking my own kids into the bathroom of the house when the storm alarm went off in our neighbourhood.

Nature can be fierce . . . raging storms like this occur and have occurred many times throughout the earth's history and especially in areas like Oklahoma . . . When I lived there, my neighbours referred to it as . . . Tornado Alley . . .

Storms can be intense and less intense depending on the weather conditions around the storm occurrence . . . this is NOT God punishing us or straightening things out in our lives . . . come on!

Are they signs of the times? . . . very possibly because the Bible is clear that in the last days these things will happen . . . in greater occurrence . . . but does that mean GOD is doing them??

If we want to see God in the midst of the storm . . . then we need to look for the responders . . . those who come to bring help and healing . . . those who bring aid and prayers and love to those who have lost so much. We need to see the partners in relief and restoration . . . These are the "visible and tangible agents" of God's grace and love. We need to see the "church" the "family of God" shining with His light and love . . .

61

How much more do we bring pain ... and anguish and division when we repeat thoughtless statements that make God look terrible ... saying this was God's hand bringing justice? But sometimes it is ...

It's certainly true ... that we need to change and yield to the Spirit of God in becoming all that He wants us to be ... but He loves us ... He is our Father ... He is always for us ... He is not an "angry God" seeking retribution ... retaliation and punishment ... He is a loving God seeking the best for us ...

In the midst of the storms of life ... God is seeking to use all that the enemy means for evil, for good ... He is using all that happens to us ... to better us ... change us ... to shift our thinking and transform our lives ...

God is GOOD ... ALL the time ... and ALL the time ... God is GOD!!!

There is however a "spiritual storm" brewing. Since Israel has been back in her own land ... we have seen an explosion in technology and travel ... we are definitely living in the "Information Age."

Constantly ... there are wars and rumours of wars. There has been a "drastic increase" in the intensity of "natural disasters" ... and in the last few years ... these disasters have even become a threat to the global food supply.

Immorality is definitely on the rise ... with legalized abortion and homosexual marriage ... in addition we have a rising state of sex outside of marriage ... a whole counterfeit covenant of "common law" unions and ongoing situations of adultery and divorce.

Hedonism and the fleshly desire to "have it all" at any cost ... has led the world into a desperate credit crisis ... which is threatening to collapse economies all around the world ... Can we really blame God ... for the mess we are in?

He told us what to expect in these days ... BUT we also "know" that HE is committed to us and to seeing us experience "His best" in the midst of what is going on in the world . . . Fear not for He has overcome the world and in Him so shall we overcome! We may be "in" the world . . . but . . . we are NOT "of" the world . . .

We are "of His Kingdom" and we are called as believers to bring heaven to bear on earth in our "words" and "deeds" Time for the church . . . to "practice what we preach"

Luke 21:25-28—"And there will be signs in the sun, in the moon, and in the stars; and on the earth distress of nations, with perplexity, the sea and the waves roaring; men's hearts failing them from fear and the expectation of those things which are coming on the earth, for the powers of the heavens will be shaken. Then they will see the Son of Man coming in a cloud with power and great glory. Now when these things begin to happen, look up and lift up your heads, because your redemption draws near."

CHAPTER 21

Our Word In Action

Many "believers" are walking in deception today . . . because they "do not walk" in the Word! . . . and they do not walk in their "own" word either . . .

They "say" they will do something . . . however we do not "see" what they "say" . . . and they end up eating the fruit of their "own way" . . . we see them "isolate" or "re-locate" because they choose to take . . . satan's bait!

Many are making concessions for "their flesh" . . . they are giving the devil place by embracing offence and they "are deceived" into believing they are still Ok spiritually . . . The Bible says clearly that walking in the flesh always brings corruption. Only when we walk in the Spirit do we walk in true freedom . . .

Our flesh will keep us in bondage to self . . . When we are "self-conscious"

we cannot be "God-conscious" . . . because in this state we are much more interested in and focused on pleasing "self" . . . than God . . .

Pride is the major cause of "being offensive" and of "taking offence."

How dare "they" do that to ME . . . How dare "they" say that to ME . . . When we embrace and operate in offence . . . we enter into the place of "defence" and quickly we move to discord . . . division . . . and deception!

Our "pride" will keep us from making things right . . . it will keep us from humbling ourselves . . . and operating by the spirit of God. It will keep us "self righteous" and unwilling to yield to doing what is "really right" . . . in the eyes of God.

You see God gives "grace to the humble" . . . but He "resists the proud." The Bible says that God "hates" pride . . . Many today, opt out of their appointed place because they are too prideful to admit they were wrong . . . and they need to change like everyone else . . .

We must hate the pride in our own lives . . . it's time to humble ourselves and focus on what God wants . . . not what we want . . . to do things His way . . . to exercise our will in compliance to Him . . . As believers we should never exercise our will contrary to God . . . We "know" what is right and wrong . . . so we cannot plead ignorance when we choose to walk contrary to His Word and way . . . When we do . . . we allow our flesh to decide and we take the side of the enemy . . .

The devil loves nothing better than when we allow our flesh to partner with him and we choose to act in ways that are contrary to the Word of God! We score lots of points through the goal posts of the darkness . . . when we refuse as believers to walk in the love and Word of God . . .

The "world" looks at us in distaste and disgust when they "see" that we do not "practice what we preach" They "see" that we "say" we walk in love . . . but we really only "talk" we don't really walk . . . the Bible says they will "know" us by the "love" we have for one another . . . Our love must be evident and tangible . . . in our words and in our deeds!

Today more than ever people are "watching us." They are "looking to see" if we live out . . . what we "say" we believe . . .

Do what you say
if you really believe
This guarantees that
You won't be deceived . . .

Don't "say" that you will
And then . . . be a spiritual fake
A true believer is known
By the action he takes . . .

Let's be doers of the Word . . . not hearers only . . . deceiving ourselves . . .
Let's really be those who "walk in" the Word . . . and love of God.
Let's be "real-deal" Christians reflecting the life of Christ in the darkness of the
world today . . . and also allowing our light to shine in the house of The Lord and
with our brothers and sisters in the family of God!

Let our love be evident and tangible
that others may truly "see"
Jesus living out His life . . .
Through you and me . . .

Let's be true examples
operating in ALL His ways . . .
In everything we "do"
And everything we "say"!

Our "life" . . . not our "lips" really tells the story . . . Our words should be a true
expression of a submitted life . . . a life given over to Jesus . . . a life laid down and
poured out for others . . . Words . . . can be cheap . . . Actions . . . really speak . . . !

CHAPTER 22

Knowledge Understanding and Wisdom

The Bible says we perish for lack of knowledge . . . but when knowledge comes . . . it brings understanding and life!!!

Apostle Paul said . . . this one thing I do . . . forgetting those things that are behind . . . and reaching forth to those things which are before me . . . reaching for the prize of the high calling of God in Christ Jesus . . .

If we do not "separate ourselves" from the principalities and powers we were born under . . . and "marry ourselves" to Jesus and His Kingdom principalities and powers . . . then we will always return to behaving the same "old" way . . . we may change for a season . . . but we will always revert back to the "old" . . . when we experience challenges . . . troubles and opposition. Each one of us was born under "family traditions" . . . beliefs . . . customs . . . and "inherited behavioural patterns" . . . things that have no place in the culture of the Kingdom of God.

People who do not understand Kingdom Culture will not understand this . . . and will be offended at these sayings . . . but our traditions and culture are an enemy to God!

There is nothing wrong with celebrating our authenticity and our ethnic character . . . but if we are saved we are citizens of another Kingdom and we must embrace the culture of the King!

Separating ourselves from "wrong roots" will allow our living tree to bear new fruit . . . as we attach ourselves to the vine . . . to the word and the will of God . . . We will find that this is a spiritual thing . . . that allows us to grow up into the fullness of the life force of heaven . . .

It's the "old" stuff that keeps us in bondage . . .

In Africa some still give a cow as a dowry . . . because they understand Baal . . . the presidents still go under the water . . . and kill something . . . like a goat or a chicken and they drink the blood . . . They are still in captivity to the principalities they were born under "generationally" . . . We must take authority over the roots of the Nation . . . not the branches . . . but pull the entire tree out by the roots and re-plant a planting of The Lord!!

We must take authority over the roots in our own lives . . . We can still have temper issues . . . and be operating a healing ministry at the same time. We are mixed . . . because we take off branches but we do not lay an axe to the root . . .

When knowledge and understanding comes . . . freedom can follow . . . when we will do the things we need to do and then walk in it!!

"MY People" perish for lack of knowledge . . .

Let's get knowledge . . . and with it . . . wisdom and understanding!

CHAPTER 23

Miracle Out of a Mess

Negative circumstances do not negate God's will

It's good to know that our circumstances do not determine whether or not God is with us, and directing the affairs of our lives.

The Bible declares that The Lord was with Joseph . . . through all of the great testings and trials. Through every life situation . . .

Joseph found favour in the sight of God . . . Joseph suffered at the hands of others . . . and ultimately at the hand of God . . . Nothing happens to us . . . that God does not allow . . . Everything in our life as believers is Father filtered!

When Joseph served in Potiphar's house it was with a "joyful attitude" and a "willing spirit" . . . and because he did not give into the demands of Potiphar's vindictive wife . . . she falsely accused him . . . He was trying to do the right thing and serve in the way God had commanded him to and when he refused to do this terrible thing and sin against God and Potiphar . . . she became scorned and rejected and set herself up as an enemy to Joseph . . . and ultimately to the plan of God.

When she spoke "these accusations" others believed her and Joseph was punished for something he did not do . . . Her attitude of "wanting what she wanted" set her up to be bitter and unfulfilled . . . and because Joseph did not give in . . . she came against him . . .

And the house of Potiphar suffered as Joseph was removed . . .

BUT The Lord was with Joseph . . . every set back and demotion became a set up and promotion . . . NO one and nothing can stop the plan of God in our lives . . .

The tactics of the devil . . . can only hinder . . . they can never bring to no affect the purposes and will of God in a life that is given over to Him.

They will be fulfilled if we "continue to move forward" and "not be stopped" by the devil and his plot to derail the plan of God in our lives . . . our city . . . our Nation . . .

The only thing that can stop the plan and purpose of God for our lives . . . is US . . . WE choose . . . it's our decision if we will serve The Lord or serve ourselves . . . if we will answer the call or do our own thing . . . if we will do what's right or cave into pressure from others . . .

We need to see the big picture . . . God's ultimate plan for Joseph was to reconcile a family . . . to save a generation and . . . to deliver a people from famine and death . . . When God does something . . . it is with the big picture in mind . . .

The momentary challenges that we go through are not stumbling blocks but stepping stones to something much greater . . . someplace higher and deeper in the plan and purpose of God . . .

Joseph started out as his Father's favourite . . . loved and valued . . . but hated and despised by his brothers . . . jealousy and bitterness caused them to overtake him and cast him into a pit . . . then they sold him to be a slave . . . taking his coat from him and using it to deceive their Father . . . telling him Joseph was killed by a wild animal.

But none of this stopped God from making Joseph into the deliverer He planned he would be . . . because nothing stopped Joseph from continuing to trust in and believe God to deliver him . . .

No matter what the circumstances of our life are today . . . we can praise our way out of prison . . . we can decide to become the one who brings salvation and deliverance to others and we can go from the pit to the palace if we keep our attitude right and keep our heart and our eyes set on God alone! He will do whatever He promised to . . . and we will receive . . . if we dare to believe . . .

CHAPTER 24

Moving Forward

Today in my quiet time with The Lord . . .

I saw old things in a closet . . . instead of cleaning it out . . . I saw people kept moving them into the back . . . There was a "hoarding" spirit that was re-arranging things . . . to keep them.

Then I heard the sound of change . . . it was like a wind and a whistle. I saw the harvest . . . but I felt a great heat . . . I saw a family reunion . . . it was good . . . but it was the same old . . . same old . . . Then I saw a move forward . . . a letting go and a taking hold . . . and a gathering in . . .

I heard the Lord say the old was good but it will keep you from my best . . . cherish your roots . . . respect your foundations but get ready to move and build . . .

We have to let go . . . in order to take hold . . . the desire to move on has to be greater than the desire to hold on . . . let go and take hold . . .

Changes . . . and challenges . . . bring growth . . .

Right before a major breakthrough sometimes we feel like having a major break down . . . the heat is always the hottest before the harvest . . .

Cherish the memories but not at the expense of making new ones . . .

Mix and mingle . . . is the unity jingle . . .

I saw some storm clouds
I saw the hand of God moving them away
I saw people rising up and His hand take hold of hands stretched out
I saw a strobe light searching and shining

JUST TO PONDER NOT TO PREACH

Do not be weary in well doing
For in due season you shall see
The fruits of your labour
As you keep your eyes on me . . .

I'm the Alpha and Omega
The beginning and the end
I am always with you
Your everlasting friend

No matter what it looks like
No matter how it seems
Keep your focus on my promise
And your heart upon the dream

For I am doing something
I am building a team
I am working with you
And behind the scenes . . .

New things are up ahead
As Old things will fall away
You are stepping up and in
To the fullness of a new day

There are voices speaking
Wrong things said and wrong things done
Just keep your focus on my plan
And your eyes upon the son . . .

For I am building something new
By my Spirit and my plan

Do not be concerned with the natural
Keep holding heavens hand

And I will build my church
And put things in perfect place
You can trust me to fulfill it
By the power of my grace

You . . . arise and shine my light
Rise up and truly be
A carrier of my truth
And a vessel of my glory

You will make a difference
When your "life" becomes My light
You can shine and show the way
For others to win this earthly fight . . .

It is your decision . . . to rise to the occasion
You are My Lighthouse by design
But you can't be a beacon
If your light don't shine!!!

CHAPTER 25

Jesus Always the Same

God is looking for "real deal" Christians . . . He is looking for fruit . . . not fruit cakes . . . not weirdo's . . . but a peculiar people . . . willing to yield to His plan . . . He touched us "with a purpose" and "for a purpose" . . .

In these days God is shaking everything that can be shaken . . . He is setting the stage for the end time move of His Spirit . . . All we have to do is pay attention to what is happening in the "natural" to understand what is happening "in the spirit realm."

God is the same . . . yesterday . . . today and forever . . . If he spoke then . . . He is speaking now . . . All of creation is awaiting the manifestation . . . the revealing of the sons of God . . . and the sons of God are those who are "led by His Spirit."

Religion and legalism are dirty words in the mouth of God . . . He is calling us to relationship and holiness . . . Be holy as I am Holy says The Lord . . . We are part of the Royal Priesthood, the company of believers . . . part of a Holy Generation . . . One day soon we will make account to Him for what we accomplished "by His spirit" and the "works of our flesh" will be burnt up in the fire . . .

A major shift has occurred . . . we don't want to get stuck where we used to be . . . stuck in old ways . . . old thoughts . . . old behaviours . . . We are called to shake up the world . . . not "fit in" but "stand out" . . .

What good is our Christianity if we never bear fruit that lasts for the Kingdom . . . So many today in the "traditional church" are full of "head knowledge" and self . . . instead of being filled with His Spirit and His purposes . . . They are so "puffed up" with what they "think they know" . . . they don't even seek God . . .

His word is clear . . . Trust in the LORD with all your heart and "lean not on your own understanding" . . . in "all your ways" acknowledge him . . . and he will direct your path . . . "Do not be wise in your own eyes" . . . fear the LORD and shun evil.

So MANY in the traditional "church" are not actively "being the church" . . . and they are wise in their own eyes . . . accepting things that are an abomination to Him . . . tolerating sin and misrepresenting the purposes of God's grace . . . questioning the ways of God . . . sceptical of His life giving and life flowing Spirit today . . . unbelieving . . . and critical of those who are pressing into the more of God . . . coming against those who are actively ministering to people and actually seeing change and transformation because the God on the inside of them is being manifest and made real.

Religion loves to criticize . . . but I've never seen a statue erected to a critic . . . but many to those who were criticized . . .

Jesus himself was criticized and ostracized by the "religious and pious" people of his day . . . there is nothing new under the sun. They are still alive and well today and continuing in the ministry of persecution of the "remnant" . . . those disciples of Christ that are still operating in the purpose and plans of God by moving in the Present Day Ministry of Jesus. His power is as real today as it was yesterday . . .

We must never justify our unbelief . . . by attacking what someone else does not believe . . .

He is the same yesterday today and forever . . .

CHAPTER 26

Trust in All Things

I saw a chess board in the heavens . . . I saw some pieces in a precarious place . . . and I saw others in a wrong place and still others completely out of place . . . I saw the wind come and turn the board upside down . . . and some of the pieces couldn't be found . . .

I heard The Lord say . . . it's time to get in place and stay in place . . . He's about to pick up the pace . . . He said its time to stand your ground don't let the wind of change knock you out or knock you down . . . For change is eminent but as you stay rooted and grounded in me . . . there will be much fruit upon your living tree . . .

Old situations will be made new and new things are on the way when you do what I've called you to today . . . There is Power in the present . . . in the moment . . . in this hour . . . Call upon my name . . . call upon my power . . . That which you have been believing for . . . is surely on the way . . . don't get discouraged . . . and miss your harvest day . . .

As you are faithful to give . . . and sow your seed . . . I promise I will meet your each and ever need . . . Covenant is my heart . . . It is my way and plan . . . I love to see you trust me to provide for you . . . by my hand . . .

Is there anything too big for me . . . says The Lord . . . is there anything my riches in glory can't afford . . . My children shall live in plenty . . . as they give according to my way . . . and they shall rise up in joy and say . . .

The blessing of the Lord maketh rich . . . and there is added no sorrow . . . I will not fear the future for God holds my tomorrow . . . I will stand by faith and I will believe . . . knowing that as I do I shall receive . . .

The enemy would try to dis-appoint you . . . from your appointment in me . . . time to open up your eyes so that you can really see . . . that the winds of change are blowing . . . and though it may feel like adversity . . . just hold fast and watch as I bring destiny . . .

The days of buying and selling and trading . . . Are coming to an end . . . But as you sow your seeds . . . Your garden . . . I shall tend . . . And as the world system falters . . . Because of the ways of man . . . You will have sown and reaped . . . according to my plan.

Don't let a field be barren . . . Continue to sow your seed . . . And as the earth experiences lack . . . You will experience ME!

Doubt sees the obstacle . . . and faith sees the way
Doubt sees the darkness . . . and faith sees the day

Doubt fears to take a step . . . while faith soars on high
Doubt questions who believes . . . and faith answers I . . . I believe.

CHAPTER 27

Be of Good Courage

God is speaking to me more and more about the power of courage in these days . . . He wants to do great things through us . . . and it will take a boldness . . . a tenacity and courage to move out in all that God has for us in this season . . . Those who possess courage . . . have a trait that will permeate and transform everything they do . . . when we have courage everything is an adventure . . . Today . . . more than ever . . . with the great tasks ahead of us . . . we need to be of good courage . . .

Josh 1:6 says, "Be strong and courageous, because YOU will lead these people to inherit the land I swore to their forefathers . . . THIS LAND, at the time was swarming with enemies . . . and today it still is . . . we live in a season where the government is implementing things in the public school that we do not agree with and they are legislating that it be mandatory for our children to participate . . . they are teaching "alternate lifestyle" and brainwashing the innocent minds of our children and youth . . . and the list goes on" . . .

In Deuteronomy, Moses told the people to be strong and courageous . . . do not be afraid or terrified because of them . . . (the enemy forces at work) . . . and for us today we cannot have fear of man operating . . . we need to move in the fear of the Lord and stand up and have the courage of our convictions . . . in 1 Chronicles . . . David told his son Solomon . . . Be strong and courageous and do the work . . . Do not be afraid or discouraged . . . That's a good word for all of us too . . . we must DO the work . . . take the steps necessary . . . and not cower in fear but rise up in faith . . . and not allow the enemy to talk us out of the place and position God has called us to occupy.

The obstacles these people faced were big . . . and seemingly never ending . . . God constantly reminded them to have courage . . . and today He is still reminding us to rise up . . . don't back down . . . be strong and of good courage . . . for the Lord your God IS with YOU!!! even though the issues we face seem so big and never ending . . .

God has not given us a spirit of timidity, but a spirit of power and love and a sound mind . . . Today IS the day . . . to STAND UP and stand firm . . . with the belt of truth buckled around our waist . . . and with the breastplate of righteousness in place . . . take up your shield of faith . . . be pleasing in His sight . . . now's the time to tear down the principalities of the night . . .

We are living in the last days . . . the devil is pulling out the stops and working in overdrive . . . thank God we KNOW that he is only "spinning his wheels" he can never stop the plan of God . . . BUT he can hinder our progress if we do not stand up and take the authority that has been given to us . . .

Jesus gave us the keys to the Kingdom . . . it's time for us to USE them to advance the Kingdom of light and quench and dispel the kingdom of darkness . . .

It is always our choice . . . what we will do . . . BUT God wants us to!!!!

CHAPTER 28

Just Believe

So many today are so afraid of being deceived by something they "might believe" that they are deceived into "believing nothing" . . .

Fear is the greatest tool that the devil uses against us . . . it can keep us from . . . witnessing . . . praying for people . . . sharing the Word . . . believing in the power of God for today . . . and it will keep us believing that the "best" things Jesus came to bring us have "passed away" . . .

The fear of "man's reproach" . . . has kept us from the fear of God . . . The fear of what "people think" about what we believe . . . keeps us from believing for more of God . . .

I spent some time this week asking people how they felt about miracles . . . and if they "did happen in the past" do they "still happen" today . . .

First I asked those who attend "traditional" churches what they thought about miracles. It seems that for many (with the exception of the Catholic church goers) miracle stories are difficult. Some say they want to believe in them, but because their church says they do not really happen today . . . they needed "proof" . . . Others said things like, I've never "seen" one . . . or . . . maybe God plays favourites so they only happen for some . . . A few did not want to dismiss them . . . just because they hadn't personally seen or experienced one . . . and they knew that didn't mean that they don't happen . . . and still others said if they don't see them . . . they are not happening . . .

People that didn't really "go to church" on the other hand . . . were all for miracles happening and in fact would welcome one in several situations they were facing right now . . . They were searching for the "living God" the God of the Bible . . . the "miracle worker" . . .

Young people ... so tired of dead religion and the hypocrisy in the church are look-ing for real Christianity ... they are longing to see the real Jesus ... the authentic Jesus ... searching for the power and authority that the Bible states He gave "us" ... they want the Power of God to "truly" be revealed ...

The group that believe in miracles ... believe also in the baptism of the Holy Spirit and the "present day power" of God ... they shared great things that God had done for them physically, financially, in protection from bad things happening and through answered prayers for their families ...

I'm sure that it was just as difficult for those who did not "see" the miracles that Jesus performed ... to believe ... I'm almost certain that there were many nay say-ers when the disciples told the stories of their "experiences" with Jesus ... and the Bible is clear that the "religious leaders" of the day accused Jesus of operating by the power of the devil ...

Just imagine if you heard this story today ... would you believe ... ?

Mark 4:35-41
Jesus is in a boat with his disciples ... he's having a snooze in the stern when a fierce storm blows up ... the waves were threatening to sink the boat ... and the disciples ... were scared. They called to him waking him up and saying ... don't you care if we drown ... He comes out and rebukes and calms the storm.

The imagery in this story is fantastic: Here they are in the dark of night out in a boat with death knocking at their door, the storm is fierce and their fear is great ... At the sound of their great distress and need ... Jesus awakes and speaks to the wind and the waves and calms the storm ... showing them his "power." He controls the forces of nature and keeps them all safe. This is a sure sign to the disciples that God is with them, and they are in awe of the miracle working Jesus ...

Would we believe this story if we heard that it happened today ... or would we ac-cuse those that said it happened of making a big hoopla over nothing ... Would we dismiss and disregard it . . . just because we didn't see it? Or would we be those that would insist that these things only happened with Jesus and they don't happen anymore . . .

As Christians we should be careful of the "judgments" we make when we are expressing our opinions . . . about what God will and will not do . . . today . . .

Jesus lives in the hearts of all of us who call Him Lord . . . in some . . . He "sleeps" waiting for us to call out for Him . . . and awaken Him like the disciples did that night on the storm tossed seas. His Spirit is longing to come awake within us to give us courage and hope . . . to show each one of us the way. If we can learn to arouse by faith the Spirit that resides . . . inside . . . then maybe miracles wouldn't be so rare or random. I propose that they would be happening in greater measures . . . Jesus did say that "we" would do greater works . . .

A miracle is a surprising and welcome event . . . that is not explained by natural or scientific laws and is considered to be divine . . . like the day our grandson woke up after being on life support with "no hope" (the Dr. said) . . . It was definitely a surprising and "very welcome" event when after five days of trusting and standing in faith . . . the young man who the Dr. Said had "no hope" opened his eyes. Thank you Lord . . . I will continue to believe you . . . I will continue to believe that with you . . . ALL things are possible!!

Matthew 19:26, Luke 1:37, Mark 9:23 Mark 10:27, Luke 18:27 . . .

CHAPTER 29

God's Love

This morning God is speaking to me about the "power" of operating in the God kind of love . . . I was in the book of John in the 4th chapter . . . starting in the 7th verse . . .

My beloved friends, let us continue to love each other since love comes from God. Everyone who loves is born of God and experiences relationship with God. The person who refuses to love doesn't know the first thing about God, because God is love—so you can't know him if you don't choose to love. This is how God showed his love for us . . . God chose to send his only Son into the world so we might live through him. This is the kind of love I'm talking about . . . the "active" love that sent his own Son as a sacrifice to take away "our sins" and make a way for us to be reconciled to the Father.

My dear, dear friends, if God loved us "like this" . . . we certainly ought to actively love each other . . . No one has seen God . . . but if we love one another, then God dwells deeply within us, and "his love" becomes apparent to those around us . . . and as we choose to practice His love . . . it becomes complete in us . . .

The Bible says that the "love of God" . . . His agape love . . . HAS BEEN shed abroad in "our hearts" by the Holy Spirit. We have it . . . but it does us no good if we do not appropriate it and apply it when human love fails . . .

Human love . . . is a funny thing. We love ice cream . . . cars . . . clothes . . . and music groups . . . We love using the word "love" . . . Have we "used" this word in so many different situations that it has lost the power of its original meaning . . . What does it "really mean" . . . to love? Does "saying" you love someone really mean that you do . . . and do we really understand the power of real love . . .

Faith by itself, if it is not accompanied by action, is dead. It's great to "believe" something . . . but if you never "act" on what you believe . . . then who's to say you "really believe." Our faith is evidenced first by our words . . . but it is confirmed by our action . . . I believe that when it comes to loving someone . . . it's the same principle . . . who's to "say" you really love someone unless you "show" them your love with your actions.

God is calling us to action . . . in our faith walk . . . and our love walk . . . the two work and walk together . . . it takes faith . . . to love some people . . . but it's a choice we make because love is of God . . . and if we love Him . . . we will love others . . . He loved us while we were "still" sinners . . . so we are called to show God's love to ALL people . . .

The Bible says that "faith" works by "love" . . . If we are not walking in love then the Word of God says our faith is "NOT" working . . . let's begin to press into the full operation of God's love . . . the love that loves "in spite of" and not "because of" . . . the love that is unconditional . . . There is nothing we can "do" today to make God love us more . . . and nothing we can do to make Him love us less . . .

I saw Jesus as he came to the waters of baptism that day . . . there came a voice from heaven . . . and I heard the Father say . . . I am "well pleased" in this "my son" not because of a single thing He's done . . .

Jesus' ministry had not even started yet . . . God's love was not based on His performance . . . that's true . . . and neither is God's love for me and you!!!

Let's learn to give and receive God's love . . . and let it become perfected in us as we allow it to flow in and through us . . .

CHAPTER 30

Let Adoption be the Option

The Bible does not specifically address the issue of abortion. There are, however, numerous Scriptures that make it abundantly clear what God's view of abortion is. Jeremiah 1:5 tells us that God knows us "before" He forms us in the womb.

Psalm 139:13-16 speaks of God's active role in our creation and "formation in the womb." Exodus 21:22-25 prescribes the same penalty—for someone who causes the "death of a baby in the womb" as for someone who commits murder. This clearly indicates that God considers a baby in the womb to be "as human" as an adult. For believers . . . abortion is not a matter of a woman's right to choose . . . It is a matter of the "life or death" of a human being made in God's image (Genesis 1:26-27; 9:6).

The first argument that always arises against the Christian stance on abortion is "What about cases of rape and/or incest"? As horrible as this would be to become pregnant as a result . . . is the abortion of the baby really the right answer? Two wrongs do not make a right. The child . . . who is a result of this terrible crime could be given in adoption to a loving family unable to have children of their own. The baby is completely innocent and should not be punished for the evil acts of someone else . . .

The second argument that usually arises is "What about when the life of the mother is at risk"? This is the most difficult question to answer on the issue of abortion. Let's hear the facts first . . . that "this situation" is the reason behind less than "one-tenth of one percent" of the abortions done in the world today.

Far more women have an abortion for convenience than women who have an abortion to save their own lives . . . Second, let's remember that we are dealing with God. He can preserve the life of a mother and a child despite all the medical odds being against it. Any couple facing this extremely difficult situation should pray to the Lord for wisdom (James 1:5) as to what He would have them to do.

Over 95 percent of abortions performed today involve women who simply do not want to have a baby. Less than 5 percent of abortions are for the reasons of rape, incest, or the mother's health at risk. Even in the more difficult 5 percent of instances, abortion should never be the first option. The life of a human being in the womb is worth every effort made to allow the child to be born . . . Let "adoption" be the option!!

For those who have had an abortion, this sin is no less forgivable than any other sin. Through faith in Christ, ALL sins can be forgiven (John 3:16; Romans 8:1; Colossians 1:14).

A woman who has had an abortion, a man who has encouraged an abortion, or even a doctor who has performed one—can all be forgiven by faith in Jesus Christ. Thank God!!

CHAPTER 31

There's Power in Your Place

I heard the Lord say . . . Where are my chosen vessels?
Where are those that I have spoken to . . . to stay the course . . .
Where are the ones I hand picked for this season and day
Where am I in their priority order and plan?
Am I at the mercy of the plans of man . . . ?

Don't be at the airport . . . when your ship comes in . . .

Many are misplaced . . . displaced and out of place . . . to the place of disgrace . . .

There is power "in your place" . . . your place physically . . . and the right place in
your heart . . .

Many are "doing their own thing" in this season . . . they are called according to
the purpose and plan of God . . . but they are "out of place" . . . the mighty men of
Joel's army did not break rank . . . they were not "missing in action" and they did
not disobey orders and move in rebellion . . . As those called by God, are we staying
in place?

This is a strategic season and time . . . God is aligning and preparing His people for
the next level and season . . . but many are not "in place" for the promotion.

I saw more ground breaking happening . . . and a greater work of God coming forth . . . I saw people diligently helping and explosions were happening all
around . . . It was bringing about the purposes and plans of the Kingdom . . . I saw
others mulling around but not really that interested . . . like they weren't sure it was
coming that soon so they had time to waste . . . many others did not appreciate the
place they were in . . . and took advantage of the situation . . . or only entered in . . .
if it fit their schedule . . . and still others that were called were off doing their own

thing . . . having lost sight of their "inheritance" . . . as new faces . . . eager and hungry for God . . . were stepping right up and into an "empty place."

This is the enemy's plan . . . to distract us from our place . . . or offend us in our place . . . to make us dissatisfied in our place . . . so we will step out of place . . . The Lord told me some are "physically" in place . . . but their "heart is out of place" . . . they are not willing to restore and reconcile in the place they have been called to . . . they are serving with their lips . . . but where is their heart?? God is "expecting" us as believers . . . to "walk in the ministry of reconciliation" so . . . how much more as "Ministers and Pastors"? . . . and rightly so . . . if we can't . . . then should we really be at the head of a congregation and preach a word we cannot practice?

There is a testing of The Lord in this season to see where our heart is . . . The plum line has dropped and The Lord is weighing hearts in a whole new way as He takes us to a whole new place . . . today more than ever, we need to ask ourselves . . . am I serving God . . . or self? Is He first . . . or did I shift my priorities??

I saw a chess board
I saw some pieces in precarious places . . .
And I saw others in a wrong place and still others completely out of place
I saw the wind of the Spirit come and turn the board upside down . . . and some of the pieces couldn't be found . . .

I hear The Lord say . . . it's time to get in place and stay in place . . . He's about to pick up the pace . . . He said it's time to stand your ground don't let the wind of change knock you out or knock you down . . . For change is eminent and it will bring a freshness to the vision and new life . . . to old things . . .

Old situations will be made new and new things will become comfortable and fit when you are willing to do what I've called you to . . . things that you have been believing for are surely on the way . . . don't get discouraged and miss your harvest day . . . covenant is my heart . . . it is my way and plan . . . I love to see my people walking hand in hand . . . the enemy would try to dis-appoint you from your appointment in me . . . time to open up your eyes so that you can really see . . . that the winds of change are blowing and though it may feel sometimes like adversity . . . but just hold fast and watch as I bring destiny . . .

God showed me that . . . Things are happening quickly in this new season . . . God's provision for the vision is "here" . . . Now is the time to be in place . . . press in and receive . . . The days and years sown in the foundational place have been well spent for we are now building on a solid structure that was revealed and birthed in the heart of God . . . In the next two years many will be lured away by the enemy if we are not aware of his tactics . . . and many other lives will be enriched because of what the Lord is doing now . . . in five years we will be amazed at what God has done . . .

The past 10 years have been incredible . . . but we are in the days of acceleration and increase . . . and God is picking up the pace . . . don't miss your God opportunity by being "Out of Place"!

CHAPTER 32

Our Words

Our words are carriers of power. They are vessels from heaven . . . or hell. They bring blessings or curses . . . depending on how we "choose to use" them. Our words are creative and call things that be not as though they are or they are destructive as we negatively speak over issues in our lives agreeing with the enemy that things will never change.

God spoke the world into existence and we speak our world into existence too . . . good or bad it's up to me and you . . . the power of our words . . . bring death or they bring life . . . they bring solution . . . or they bring strife . . . they bring health and healing . . . or darkness and despair . . . we speak words of encouragement or our words say, I don't care . . . our words can change the situation . . . or add darkness to the day . . . We always must be mindful . . . of the things we say . . . for the power of life and death . . . we chose when we speak . . . do we want things our way . . . or is it His will that we seek . . . He has given us such power . . . to bring faith and light . . . it's up to us to order our conversation right . . . to speak words that are gracious and keep them short and sweet . . . we never know how many . . . we might have to eat!!

Proverbs . . . 12:18
"There is one who speaks like the piercings of a sword . . . but the "tongue of the wise" promotes health. The "truthful lips" shall be established forever, but a lying tongue . . . is but for a moment."

Isaiah 50:4
"The Lord God has given me the tongue of the learned, that I should know how to speak a word in season to him who is weary."

Proverbs 16:24
"Pleasant words are like a honeycomb, sweetness to the soul and health to the bones."

Proverbs 15:4 . . . "A wholesome tongue is a tree of life"
Proverbs 10:11 . . . "The mouth of a righteous man is a well of life"
Proverbs 10:21 . . . "The lips of the righteous feed many"

You can "raise your words" without "raising your voice"
It's the rain that causes the flowers to grow . . . not the thunder!!

CHAPTER 33

Guard Your Heart

The same sun that melts the ice, will harden the clay.

A work of God can bring about two completely different responses, depending on the condition of a persons heart . . . You are what your heart is . . .

Proverbs 23:7 . . . For as a man thinks in his heart, so is the man . . .
Proverbs 27:19 As in water face reflects face, so a man's heart reveals the man.

If a person's heart is not in a good place, then when God moves on a situation or in someone else's life and on their behalf . . . anger, resentment, jealousy, envy, rebellion, and eventually bitterness can set in. This causes a hardening of the heart in the person who is responding in the wrong spirit. Love will wax cold as they receive a "fiery dart", then they fall away and their lives will fall apart.

Bitterness sets in like a disease and slowly infests the heart and takes us out of the position of blessing . . .

But when we remain in a place of humility, and God moves, we will be provoked to joy, celebration, anticipation and expectancy . . . We will celebrate the process of God in the lives of others and have a healthy expectation of Him moving in our own life. We will honour others. We will live in obedience to God . . . and we will be open to receive the next level of promotion in our journey with Him.

Let's keep watch over and guard the condition of our heart that the Son will continue to melt away any issues that would come to harden us and make us bitter and resentful. May the light and the warmth of the Son continue to keep the flame of our love warm and burning bright . . . that we would be an example of humility and grace to others.

Let's not end up like King Herod and because of our unwillingness to do what God wants us to do . . . and do what's right to do . . . our heart becomes un-yielded and hardened. Because of pride and self righteousness we can become puffed up and begin to operate outside of the will and Word of God and we will practice self will . . . and have a selfishness attitude instead of being in His will and operating out of a selfless attitude. We will become deceived and begin to operate out of offence and division and we will fall away in our heart and then our life will fall apart.

Guard your heart for out of it flows all the issues of your life.

CHAPTER 34

Being Family

When we truly begin to see the "body of Christ" like a family . . . we will not so easily forsake those God has called us to work with . . . to bring salvation, healing and deliverance to the world . . . A sense of "true family" will give us the spirit to fight together no matter what . . .

God intended for "church" to be a family . . . with members working, walking and worshipping together "in love" not being willing to walk away from the family because of selfish desires . . . fleshly excuses . . . or thinking more highly of ourselves than other family members . . .

It takes humility to be part of a family . . . and be willing to walk with our brothers and sisters to infiltrate the kingdom of darkness with HIS marvelous love and light . . . God is looking for "internal integrity" in the family of God today . . . He does not want us to practice "spiritual adultery" but to stand with one another committed and in covenant.

HE chose our family for us in the "natural" and also "in the spirit" . . . Sanctification comes through habitation . . . The biggest obstacle we have to overcome . . . is "ourselves" . . . The biggest room for improvement in the "house" is self improvement . . .

Whatever we are going through today . . . whatever issue . . . choices . . . obstacles or problems . . . God is using it . . . to test us . . . and to see and show us where we are in maturity and readiness for ministry to others. Many are held back from ministry because of lack of maturity and the inability to walk in forgiveness, reconciliation, and restoration.

There are "no good excuses" in God to leave our covenant place . . . Lots of people do it . . . in marriage . . . in family . . . in church . . . but we will all stand before God and answer for it when our works are proven at the judgment seat of Christ.

It's our "petty differences" and "preferences" that keeps us from fulfilling the high call of God in our own lives . . . God will not be mocked . . . whatever a man "sows" that shall he "also reap." We open doors into our lives for the enemy to work through our wrong attitudes, behaviors and conversations . . .

We perish because of lack of knowledge. When we really understand how our "own actions" allow the enemy to have access into our lives we will learn to "order our conversations rightly" we will "teach our mouth" to speak right things . . . we will see the truth in "as a man thinks in his heart" . . . so is the man, and we will renew our minds . . . in the Word and allow it to change us realizing that Ministry . . . is about LOVE . . .

Our purpose is to wash one another's feet . . . Jesus came to serve . . . not "self serve" . . . not to "criticize" how others serve . . . But to be the example and lead in serving . . .

Lord . . . Help us to become the leaders and family members you want us to be . . . and to let go of our natural carnal behaviors . . . that we might walk in your supernatural love, compassion and power today . . . realizing that leadership is not a "position" but an "action" and we must lead by example.

CHAPTER 35

Unrealistic Expectations

Unrealistic expectation is the root of all heartache . . .

Why do people look at the world and expect something from it. Do we feel it owes us something. Today there is such a sense of entitlement, instead of empowerment. Life is still what "we" make it . . . We are in charge of charting the course of our own lives . . . and it should not be contingent on anyone else . . . there should not be a person in our lives that we are co-dependent on for our personal fulfillment.

We have a society drowning in a culture of "happily ever after." We read books . . . watch movies . . . become addicted to television shows, and we believe the lie that we will have that too . . . and instead of living our lives by the Word of God we endeavor to "produce" the fantasy of the perfect life . . . through our own actions . . . decisions . . . and willful behavior . . .

Many times we blame the consequences of our choices on someone else . . . citing that "they" failed us . . . they didn't "help us enough" . . . they didn't "teach us enough" . . . "spend enough time" with us . . . or "care enough." Then we react in anger and irritation toward those in relationship with us . . . because we blame them for the way "our life" is going . . . We are free to make our own decisions, but we are not free from the consequences of those decisions . . . good or bad . . . it's "our choice."

Disagreements in relationship are not only normal but . . . if constructively resolved . . . can actually strengthen the relationship. It is inevitable that there will be times of sadness, tension and even outright anger. The source of these problems usually lies in unrealistic or unreasonable demands . . . unreasonable expectations and unresolved issues and or behaviours from past experience or history.

Resolving conflicts requires honesty and a willingness to consider that your perspective may not be based in truth . . . but in a veiled conception of what was and is real. All of the circumstances we live through are also "filtered" through our past experiences. We must stop letting the past dictate the future, and steal the present day reality of our lives.

This one thing I do . . . letting go of what lies behind and reaching for the high call that is in Christ Jesus . . . We must "let go" of the old if we want to "take hold" of the new.

CHAPTER 36

Transition

It's still transition time. All over the Kingdom of God and throughout the Church the word of the hour is still "transition."

We are all in transition . . . so don't be surprised if my transition spills over and affects yours.

I believe God is telling His whole body to step forward. In those steps . . . we'll probably step on each other's feet. I imagine there may be a few of us pushing and shoving . . . some of us wanting to move forward while others will stand still or . . . even move backwards.

Let's face it . . . God's will is always to change us. He is always transforming us and molding and making us into something different than we are right now . . .

He is still the potter and we are His clay. This is an easy image for us to visualize and see . . . A lump of clay is shaped into a vessel by the hands of the potter and then refined in the fire until it is becomes purified and hardened. Only then is this vessel worthy of use.

Change is never comfortable but it is a "fact of life" and it is the "will of God." We are changed as we grow in age and maturity. We are changed through the passage of time and the tests and trials of life . . . We are changed when we accept Jesus into our hearts . . . and make a decision to serve Him . . . no matter what . . . and we are changed as we move into deeper relationship with God and accept His will in our lives . . . as we die to our own . . .

God is refining us in the furnace of His grace . . . that we might be like Him and reflect His face . . . God is molding us into vessels that will carry His glory . . . and making us living epistles that will tell His story . . .

103

In this time of transition we will probably feel uncomfortable . . . as God stretches us and makes us more able and pliable and flexible and teachable. Change is a good thing and it is God's will.

We all have plans for the future and goals to achieve . . . but His purposes and plans are better than we could ever believe . . .

"You can make many plans, but the Lord's purpose will prevail."
Proverbs 19:21

If we are truly given over to The Lord and our will is yielded to Him . . . then His purposes are going to come to be no matter what . . .

We need to be patient with each other as never before. We're going to have to bear one another's burdens and be willing to overlook each others faults. We're going to have to learn to let those very real hurts and offences go quickly. We're going to have to respond in love instead of reacting out of spite.

God's Word says He is returning for a Church without spot or wrinkle. How will we ever be that Church without going through the fire of refinement? We must press in and press through.

Transition is the word of the hour and humility is the path to unity and peace. If we act out of humble hearts we will demonstrate to each other and to God that we are the people He wants us to be . . . then Jesus will be glorified and then the world will see a group of loving and united believers fulfilling their destiny.

In this time of transition we will probably feel uncomfortable . . . as God stretches us and makes us more able and pliable and flexible and teachable. Change is a good thing and it is God's will.

We all have plans for the future and goals to achieve . . . but His purposes and plans are better than we could ever believe . . .

"You can make many plans, but the Lord's purpose will prevail."
Proverbs 19:21

If we are truly given over to The Lord and our will is yielded to Him . . . then His purposes are going to come to be no matter what . . .

We need to be patient with each other as never before. We're going to have to bear one another's burdens and be willing to overlook each other's faults. We're going to have to learn to let those very real hurts and offences go quickly. We're going to have to respond in love instead of reacting out of spite.

God's Word says He is returning for a Church without spot or wrinkle. How will we ever be that Church without going through the fire of refinement? We must press in and press through.

Transition is the word of the hour and humility is the path to unity and peace. If we act out of humble hearts we will demonstrate to each other and to God that we are the people He wants us to be . . . then Jesus will be glorified and then the world will see a group of loving and united believers fulfilling their destiny.

Now is the time of the harvest . . . Be encouraged!! It's promotion time!! But we must enter in like never before. We must be servants one to another. Living a life worthy of our calling and fighting the fight of faith . . .

Now is the time of the harvest . . . Be encouraged!! It's promotion time!! But we must enter in like never before. We must be servants one to another. Living a life worthy of our calling and fighting the fight of faith . . .

Philippians 2 says,
"Is there any encouragement from belonging to Christ . . . Any comfort from his love . . . Any fellowship together in the Spirit . . . Are your hearts tender and sympathetic . . . Then make me truly happy by agreeing wholeheartedly with each other . . . loving one another . . . and working together with one heart and purpose. Don't be

selfish . . . don't live to make a good impression on others . . . Be humble, thinking of others as better than yourself. Don't think only about your own affairs, but be interested in others, too, and what they are doing" . . .

If we will dare to live like this then we will dare to be great in the Kingdom of Heaven . . .

For the greatest of these are the servant of all.

CHAPTER 37

Not Your Drinking Buddy

These are the days when darkness covers the earth and gross darkness the people . . . It doesn't say unbelieving people . . .

God wants us to live "under the influence" of His Spirit . . . but He's not our drinking buddy

The Lord spoke to me and said my people are sinning the sin of "familiarity" He said, I am NOT your "drinking buddy" . . . many who think they drink at the river . . . will perish in the wilderness . . . because they do not understand . . . that there is "fire" in MY river . . . the fire that refines and changes those that truly give themselves to it. You are not called to be drunk but to "live under the influence" of my Spirit . . .

Many "splash" and "play" and soak and drink . . . but consecration is the missing link . . . they want to play in the Spirit . . . but not move in my plan . . . to change and refine every woman and man . . . they want what they want . . . as they do their own thing . . . not realizing what reproach this will bring . . . for the things of the spirit are not carnal you see . . . my Spirit reproves and my power sets free . . . many are watching in this season and day . . . the things that you "do" and the things that you "say" . . . watching and wondering . . . is this really true . . . they are looking for "ME" . . . when they're looking at you . . .

WHAT are they seeing . . . what do "your actions" say? . . . are you looking for change . . . or just looking to play . . . Be filled with my Spirit . . . the dispensation of grace . . . your actions should NEVER bring reproach or disgrace . . . when you come face to face with Jesus . . . when it's all said and done . . . He's looking at your life . . . and the race you have run . . . your works "will be judged" . . . what you did for the King . . . did you answer the call . . . or do your own thing? . . . Soaking and splashing is fine now and then . . . but over and over and over again??

107

Where is "the fruit" of the time spent with me . . . it should be evident and shining for others to see . . . the days are now dark . . . and soon comes the night . . . it's time for my people to shine forth the light . . . time to get serious . . . there is much still to do . . . time to press in . . . to what I've called you to do . . . Get into the river and out of the pool . . . time for my people to stop acting the fool . . .

I like a party . . . I'm planning one now . . . a huge celebration it's coming and WOW . . . I will be honoured . . . at the marriage feast of the lamb . . . remember I'm not your "buddy" I'm the "GREAT I AM!!"

God certainly does not mind when we enjoy His manifest presence. He loves to bless us and is happy when we are touched by His Spirit. However He touches us for a purpose . . . not just so we will "feel good" but so, that we will also "do good" For we have been saved unto good works . . . that the world might "see" our works and glorify God. He definitely wants us to have an impact in the world and influence others to become children of the Kingdom. He wants us to be involved in government . . . media . . . arts and entertainment. He wants us to be a powerful agent of change in the Market Place and education as well as in the family. We are not supposed to be going around the "mountain of religion" forever . . . drunk and ineffective . . . splashing around doing nothing for God.

John 9:4 . . . We must work the works of him who sent us . . . while it is day for night is coming . . . when no one can work . . .

It's extremely important to understand the urgency of "this work" . . . "His work" . . . in the earth . . . that we are called and set apart to co-labour together with Him in . . .

God has a designated time frame . . . "while it is day" . . . we "must" work the works . . . For the night . . . the end of time on earth . . . as we know it . . . is coming and there is still much to do . . . God has called me and you . . . to be a beacon . . . shine the light . . . Rise up and be "pleasing" in His sight . . . NOW is the time . . . NOW is the day . . . for us to "show" others His will and His way . . .

II Corinthians 5:10 . . . For we must "all appear" before the "judgment seat of Christ" . . . that "everyone" may receive a "reward of the deeds done" . . . in the body, "all things" according to what he has done . . . whether "good" or "bad."

God will not be mocked . . . for whatever a man shall sow . . . that shall he also reap . . . HE is very interested in the furtherance of the Gospel . . . the advancement of His Kingdom and the legacy of "His Family Business."

Let's continue to co-labour "with Him" to see the manifestation of His Kingdom come . . . His will be done . . . In earth as it is in Heaven!!!

CHAPTER 38

Made In His Image

Genesis 1:27: God created "mankind" in his own image . . . in the image of God . . . He created "them" both male and female!

God created us, humanity, in his own image. We were made to rule and reign, and take dominion over all creation. We were created for His pleasure . . . and to manifest His likeness.

God is too big . . . and intricate . . . too magnificent to be displayed in one gender. When He saw that Adam was all alone . . . (all one) . . . He decided that was not good . . . so he put Adam to sleep and using one of his ribs he fashioned woman from within him . . . a help mate suitable . . . one to "complete" him . . . and together "we" are to reflect God.

In marriage . . . we need one another to complete the image of God . . . and to reproduce and produce fruit. Man cannot multiply without woman . . . or woman without man.

Today they can cut it anyway they want . . . but without the seed of man . . . woman cannot multiply . . . and without the egg of the woman there is no new life. He created us together to be fruitful and multiply . . .

Today we can scientifically alter and devise many ways to do what we want to as a society . . . but . . .

Today more than ever marriage as God intended is under attack. Separation, divorce, domestic abuse, common law and same sex unions . . . all the tactics of the deceiver at work to tear down that which God said was good . . . to dismantle the family . . . break covenant . . . confuse the children . . . stifle the reproduction of creation . . . and shatter the very structure of society.

As "believers" we need to stand up and stand on the Word of God. We need to reflect the face of God and His views . . . truths and sanctions. As ambassadors of Christ we need to mirror the opinions and vision of the one who sent us. Today more than ever we must rise and shine . . . be the light in the darkness and walk together for righteousness in the earth.

"We" are made in the likeness and image of God . . . Let's run our race and reflect His face!

CHAPTER 39

Moonlight to Marriage

Genesis 3:7: Then their eyes were opened and they realized they were naked.

The wedding day . . . the climatic end to dream dates . . . undivided attention and being on top of the favorite things to do list . . . and the incredible beginning of "real love."

Marriage changes our social status . . . binds us to covenant fidelity and positions us for the greatest growth ever imaginable. Two beautiful people face one another and promise to love each other unconditionally "till death do us part." Problem is . . . those two beautiful people have a past . . . they have life patterns . . . little secrets . . . sinful tendencies . . . personality quirks and flaws . . . that will definitely surface in the "comfort of binding relationship."

There is nothing like marriage to reveal the depths or the shallowness of our commitment and convictions. In the "love is blind" state of our relationship it was easy to dismiss our partners "stuff" . . . but when it's right in our face . . . and in our space . . . well we just don't have that much grace . . . All of a sudden we live with this person EVERY day and love must become much more a "choice" than a feeling.

We usually "fall in love" by chance . . . and "fall out of love" by choice . . .

Love is a choice, not always a feeling or an emotion. It's a decision we make every day. We choose to love . . . when our husband doesn't take out the garbage . . . or when our new haircut or outfit goes unnoticed . . . or when our wife takes too long getting ready and we end up late . . . or when poor financial decisions set us back . . . we can still make the decision to love.

Loving another person is not always easy. Sometimes we don't "feel like it!" Real love can't be based on feelings or emotions that are fickle and constantly changing depending on the situation or circumstance. Feelings are not always based in truth but in what's happening in the "moment." Choosing love keeps us focused on the big picture that surfaces again once feelings and emotions have been quieted.

Love is a choice . . . an action . . . and a feeling. Love is passion . . . compassion and sacrifice. Love is attraction and commitment . . . love is words . . . deeds . . . feelings and choices . . .

We begin in the "fantasy" of fairy tale love . . . but marriage opens our eyes to the reality of "scary tale" love . . . Marriage brings all of our humanness to the surface and exposes the fullness of who we are . . . to one another. Marriage is a highway . . . under construction . . . but when we will allow that highway to be paved with grace . . . we will travel a long way together in healing and wholeness and the "two shall truly become one."

Every marriage leaves the honeymoon behind and begins a life of challenges . . . struggles . . . joys . . . and pains . . . We enter in and out of seasons of conflicts and stress into times of refreshing and renewal . . .

We birth and embrace new life together and let go of old things that no longer serve us as a "couple." We continue to choose love . . . to stand in covenant and act in loving ways . . . affirming and encouraging one another as unto the Lord . . .

I give you a new commandment: that you should love one another. Just as I have loved you, so you too should love one another . . . John 13:34.

Above all things have "intense and unfailing love" for one another, for love covers a multitude of sins . . . forgives and disregards the offences of others . . . 1 Peter 4:8.

Love bears up under anything and everything that comes, is ever ready to believe the best of every person, its hopes are fadeless under all circumstances, and it endures everything . . . (without weakening) 1 Corinthians 13:7.

With God as my witness this vow I will make
To have and to hold you . . . no other to take
For rich or for poor . . . under skies grey or blue
All my days . . . I will stand by you!!!

CHAPTER 40

Live to Give

We cannot receive the blessings of God when . . . we limit ourselves to our own resources . . . God's resources are unlimited . . . and they are accessed through His principles of giving and receiving . . . There is no provision for the vision without obedience to sow into the harvest . . . and we cannot receive by faith . . . without practicing the principles of faith . . .

Proverbs 3:9-10 . . . Honour the LORD with thy substance . . . and with the "first fruits" . . . (the tithe) of "all thine increase" . . . So shall thy barns be filled with plenty, and thy presses shall burst out with new wine.

The just shall live by faith . . . and so shall our life "BE" according to our faith . . . God has called many of us to do supernatural things that need supernatural provision . . . yet we will stay in lack because we do not discern "our seed." Some believe they don't even have seed . . . yet the Bible says HE "gives seed" to the sower. We have it . . . we must discern it! Even when God is meeting our need . . . we must learn to discern the seed . . . and don't eat the seed, sow it.

One day, years back . . . I was believing God for my rent to be paid . . . I had 200.00 and I needed 750.00. I was in a service and The Lord impressed on me to sow the 200.00. Of course, I argued saying this was money for my rent . . . He said no, that's your seed . . . If it doesn't meet the need, it's your seed . . . and as you are faithful to sow it . . . in faith . . . I will bring the increase . . . and He did. The days of learning to "live by faith" were and still are thrilling and fulfilling . . . Living by faith taps us into the "limitless" resources of God . . .

We can live in our own "limited" understanding or we can open up our heart to live in a place in Him . . . that has no lack and no limit . . . He desires that we would

117

have "more than enough" to give into every good work . . . and He "delights in" the prosperity of His people!!

We love to quote the scripture Philippians 4:19: "But my God shall supply all your needs according to his riches in glory by Christ Jesus" . . . But we forget about Philippians 4:19 . . . in the context that it was written. Here Apostle Paul is giving a promise to believers "who were operating in God's principles" of "giving and receiving" and "sowing and reaping" . . . He is repeating what Jesus said in Luke 6:38 . . . "Give and it will be given to you." Receiving is the reciprocal action to our giving . . .

Paul said to the Church at Philippi, "no church shared with me concerning giving and receiving but you only" in Philippians 4:15, . . . and in V. 17 we see him explaining that it was "not because he desired a gift but he desired that fruit may abound to their account." God put sowing in place that WE might reap the harvest . . . "Kingdom business" is financed through "Kingdom Principles."

Galatians 6:7 says . . . Do not be deceived, God is not mocked; for whatever a man sows, that he will also reap . . . yet some believers today have found a way to "justify" their lack of giving and excuse themselves from following the principles given to us in the Word for prospering God's way . . . Many boast about being self made and trust in their investments . . . stocks . . . and securities, and then deceive themselves into believing they don't have an income . . . because they don't receive a "pay cheque."

Deuteronomy 8:17-18 . . . And you say in your heart, My power and the might of my hand has gotten me this wealth. But you shall remember the LORD your God: for it is he that gives you power to get wealth that HE may establish His covenant which he swore unto your fathers . . . as it is this day.

We need to remember that money is a great "servant" . . . but a lousy master. We are all stewards . . . of what God "has given us."

118

Proverbs 3:5, 9 NLT . . . Trust in the LORD with all your heart, do not depend on your own understanding . . . Honour the LORD with your wealth and with the best part of "everything" you produce.

Nothing strengthens my faith more than giving when I don't understand how in the world I possibly can do so. Giving the way God gives . . . and the way He wants us to give . . . goes beyond simple budgeting. It requires faith. It requires us to trust in Him . . . and sometimes get out "on the limb." The Word of God tells me that the more I trust and give according to His ways . . . the stronger my faith will become. The more I give . . . the more He provides me the ability to give.

"Give, and it will be given to you . . . For with the measure you use it will be measured back to you." Luke 6:38 NIV.

Giving of our money and material possessions is the only place in the Bible where God literally says . . . come on . . . "test me in this" . . .

"For where your treasure is, there your heart will be also." Matthew 6:21 NIV.

Where I put my money . . . my time . . . my efforts and talents and gifts . . . my thinking . . . my life . . . that's where my heart will be!

I want to be more like God . . . I want to be closer to God and when I give out of a heart of love and compassion . . . I find that I'm expressing God's heart . . . For He so loved the world that "He Gave" and He gave us His best and most precious possession . . . and He keeps on giving!!

Let's learn to "live to give" . . . and "give to live" the abundant life in Him!

CHAPTER 41

Active Faith

Today many "Christians" have the opinion that it's OK to live by their own standards . . . oblivious to the standard set for us in the Word of God. Many profess to believe . . . however their lives are not evidence of that belief . . . and we see many caught up in sinful behaviors that cause them to run from God . . . from the church and from other church family members. They watch from the side lines and never enter actively into the game called life abundant . . .

Others . . . want the blessings of God and want to experience the fulfillment of Biblical promises . . . but are not ordering their lives in obedience to God. They will only do what's "comfortable" or "convenient" and are not interested in "their lives" being a living sacrifice.

To be truly happy and fulfilled . . . we must examine ourselves in the "light of God's Word" and then live by it . . . not by our standard . . . our way of thinking about it . . . our limitations or desires . . . but HIS way . . . HIS word . . . HIS will . . .

The Bible says, "Your word is a lamp to guide my feet and a light for my path" (Psalm 119:105).

As we chart the course of our lives . . . through the Word of God . . . the stress and tensions of life become more bearable . . . Life comes with problems and issues but we have the answer in the blueprint for success that has been given to us in the gift of the Word of God! Our lives are governed by a great power for good and success when we live in active obedience to the Word of faith. Simple submission and obedience to God's Word releases the power to succeed and activates our lives into the "life abundant" promise that Jesus gave us . . . when He said "I have come to bring life . . . and life abundant"

Doubt cripples . . . and faith empowers . . . Faith without works is dead . . . and Faith in action brings victory!

Faith with works . . . faith in action . . . is alive . . . and brings forth the promise of God. Faith without works . . . without action becomes an unfulfilled fantasy.

When I have faith that God is leading me to do something . . . and I do not follow or act on it . . . then my faith becomes doubt. I have heard so many people say why do I always get the "same word" or "why does the word never come to pass" . . . Hello . . . we must line our lives up . . . God is looking for "our faith" and "our obedience."

As we move forward in the Word of God and become a "doer" of it . . . we will see it come to pass . . . As human beings we find it much "easier" to exercise doubt . . . Doubt keeps us from active faith.

Faith and doubt are like oil and water . . . oil contaminates and brings a film that ruins the purity of the water . . . in the same way . . . doubt . . . reinforced by our inaction . . . pollutes the purity of our faith . . . leaving it unfulfilled . . . unfit . . . and unusable. Faith activated by action . . . overpowers doubt . . . and restores the purity of the gift that obedience then brings to fruition.

Be doers of the Word and not just hearers. We love to hear the Word . . . we rejoice in what we hear . . . and then . . . we procrastinate . . . When we try to "evaluate" His Word instead of obeying it . . . our own thoughts will plants seeds of doubt . . . which brings forth a tree of procrastination . . . bearing poisonous leaves of inaction . . .

"But they delight in the law of the LORD, meditating on it day and night. They are like trees planted along the riverbank, bearing fruit each season. Their leaves never wither, and they prosper in all they do" (Psalms 1:2).

Let's "exercise active faith" today . . . waiting and procrastinating are the breeding grounds for doubt . . . When in doubt cast it out!!!

It's one thing to "wait" on His promises . . . and quite another to "sit" on the premises . . .

CHAPTER 42

The Just Shall Live by Faith

Living by faith . . . is trusting God to supply our needs . . . not our job . . . not our investments . . . interest payments . . . or securities . . . but God alone.

God is not bound by our financial limitations . . . He is not constrained by the world's economic conditions . . . He is in control of all things that we actually give Him control over . . . Whatever we hold on to . . . holds on to us . . . and whatever we "release" brings "increase."

His method of increase is . . . Proverbs 11:24 . . . One person gives freely . . . and gains even more . . . while another withholds and comes to poverty.

Proverbs 3:9 . . . Honour the Lord with your capital and sufficiency . . . and with the first-fruits of all your income.

Malachi 3:10 . . . Bring all the tithes . . . the whole tenth of your income . . . into the storehouse, that there may be food in My house, and prove Me now by it, says the Lord of hosts, if I will not open the windows of heaven for you and pour you out a blessing, that there shall not be room enough to receive it.

This is the scripture all the anti-tithers want to use to say that tithing is Old Testament . . . but it's right before the one in Malachi 4:6 . . . about the hearts of the Fathers being turned to the sons . . . that we are walking in right now!!! DUH?? . . . NOTHING in God's Word is obsolete . . . He himself watches over His Word to perform it!! . . . Not "part" of His Word . . . or "some" of His Word . . . but all of His Word . . . He is a man of His Word! If we are doers of the Word . . . trusting God to bring it to pass . . . we shall reap a harvest . . .

God taught us a real lesson in this kind of trust when we were believing for finances for the Eagle Worldwide Campground. He challenged us to adhere to

123

and operate in "His principles" for Kingdom wealth . . . and then see Him supply "according to our faith" . . . as we followed His Word in our faithful seed sowing. He showed us first hand how to receive a harvest from planting seed in fertile ground.

He showed us how to sow our finances . . . our time . . . our talents and gifts. Our lives became a sacrifice to The Lord as He began to establish in us and through us His vision and plan for us personally and for the ministry and the region.

Of course . . . it is still always our choice what we will or will not do . . . God gave us a free will . . . it's up to me and you . . . We can step back . . . or we can step in . . . we can choose to lose . . . or we can choose to win! We can give and receive . . . according to His plan . . . or trust in the natural and the ways of man. We can believe His Word . . . as we tithe and sow . . . trusting Him to cause our finances to grow . . . or we can with hold . . . for whatever the reasons . . . and walk through barren fields and fruitless seasons . . . God will not be mocked . . . this I know is true . . . whatever we will sow . . . will be multiplied back to me and you . . . We are blessed to be a blessing . . . that's His promise still today . . . when we will choose His will and we will choose His way!

Proverbs 14:12: For "there is a way that seems right to a man . . . but its end is the way of death."

We cannot depend upon what SEEMS RIGHT TO MAN . . . We must place our trust in WHAT IS RIGHT TO GOD.

There is a way that is right . . . and cannot be wrong. There is a way that leads to all the spiritual blessings we need . . . His Word is a lamp unto our feet and it will lead us in pathways right and true . . . We must choose to do what God tells us to . . . and remember as you say . . . well God never "spoke" to me . . . His Spirit and His Word . . . always agree!!

When we exercise our "right to choose" and in doing so . . . act contrary to God's Word and will . . . we should take no pride in our choice! Let's choose to walk in His Word and enjoy the blessings of obedience.

CHAPTER 43

Patience, Ain't Nobody Got Time for That

Galatians 5:22: But the fruit of the Spirit is love, joy, peace, "patience", kindness, goodness, faithfulness . . .

Patience . . . last night I prayed for that . . . What's the hold up??

When my granddaughter Ayla was little I used to "practice our patience" with her all the time . . . teaching her to exercise control over her little temper and coaching her to wait with a good attitude . . . Then one day in a long check out line while shopping . . . she tutored me in the "practice" of my own gift of patience . . . haha and a little child SHALL lead them!!

Patience is one of the great virtues that we as human beings want and admire . . . but have difficulty practicing in our daily lives. The practice of patience is forgotten or neglected in our quest for instant gratification. Patience, endurance and perseverance are strong words . . . and strong attributes of what our character needs to be made of, especially as believers . . . because it is through faith and patience that we will obtain the promises of God! We need patience but we don't like "waiting to get it" . . . and that's the only way it's achieved. Patience and endurance must be "worked within us" . . . and it is "perfected" in the midst of the trial or test . . .

James 1:2-4 . . . My brothers and sisters, when you have many kinds of troubles, you should be full of joy, because you know that these troubles test your faith, and this will give you patience. Let your patience show itself perfectly in what you do. Then you will be perfect and complete and will have everything you need."

God doesn't give us patience . . . but he does give us opportunities to perfect it in our lives . . . We are continually faced with challenges disguised as problems that are meant to work the fruit of patience into our character . . . so that our faith might be "mature" and "actively receiving" from God.

One of the best proving grounds for our Christian growth and maturity is trouble. When we go through personal trials . . . we soon discover the kind of faith we really possess. Trials not only reveal the strength and depth of our faith . . . but they also develop our character. James was written to show us that God is trying to produce in us the kind of faith that overcomes. "The trying of our faith works patience." Patience . . . is enduring faith . . . faith with staying power . . . not "fair weather faith," but faith that perseveres through the storms.

God is trying to produce in us . . . "faith that overcomes" faith that endures . . . and has staying power. He wants us to have "faith to believe" . . . "faith to receive" and "faith to maintain" . . . The devil comes to steal, kill and destroy . . . and far too many believers fall by the wayside when temptations and trials come. These situations in our lives produce an inward change, so God allows and even ordains them to build in us overcoming faith.

Each storm we face in our lives brings its blessings and each trial produces rewards. As we learn to wait and trust in The Lord through theses trying situations and circumstances, patience brings hope . . . and produces spiritual fruit . . . and causes us to receive what God has promised.

Patience teaches us to enjoy the "success of the journey" . . . rather than rushing to get to the destination . . . it strengthens our faith . . . ensures our safe arrival and gives us a sense of assurance that God is always for us and is always at work in our lives in a "personal way" in the midst of all the issues . . . trials and tests we endure in the perfecting of our lives.

Isaiah 40:31: Those who wait on the Lord shall renew their strength; they shall mount up with wings like eagles, they shall run and not be weary, they shall walk and not faint.

Patience . . . "ain't nobody got time for that!!" Hahaha

CHAPTER 44

Don't Take the Bait

There are many "potential leaders" in the preparation stage today. We need to apply the life giving truth of scripture more today then ever as the spirit of offence, the "bait of satan", is unleashed over the body of believers.

Don't be deceived into taking the bait . . . the devil knows how to fish.

We need to "know God" and "know our enemy."

Psalm 119:165: Great peace have they which love thy law: and nothing . . . in no way . . . shall offend them.

Great peace have they which "love" thy law.

What an incredible revelation this is . . . It is not that we perfectly "keep" the law . . . but we are those who "love" it . . .

As believers . . . our hearts and lives are given over to walk in obedience to His Word and precepts . . . so much so . . . that even when we are persecuted, or someone tries to offend us, we have peace . . . because we understand the truth and the empowerment that comes from the reconciling blood of Jesus and we know the power of His comforting Spirit . . . that turns everything that happens in our lives for good . . . when we love (obey) God and are called according to His purpose.

This Psalm goes on to say . . . and "nothing" shall offend them . . . NO THING shall injure them or cause offensive behaviour . . . The Bible clearly tells us that offences will come . . . but we as lovers of His law are peacemakers . . . and we are commanded to . . . neither give nor take offence.

The peace that passes "all understanding" . . . is the one which is founded upon conformity to God's will and His Word . . . it is a living and lasting one . . . and when we walk in alignment to His Word we will always walk in peace . . . no matter what is going on around us.

Philippians 4:8-9: brothers and sisters . . . whatever is true . . . whatever is noble . . . whatever is right . . . whatever is pure . . . lovely . . . and admirable . . . whatever is excellent or praiseworthy . . . "think about these things" . . . Whatever you have learned or received or heard from me . . . or seen in me . . . put it into practice . . . and the God of peace will be with you.

We must put into practice the precepts of God's Word . . . His thoughts are not our thoughts and His ways are "higher" than our ways . . . His ways always take us up and over the situation . . . and our way keeps us under the circumstance or in the middle if it . . . trying to "figure it out."

The "believer's heart" is no longer the "seat of intellect" . . . because of His sacrifice for us . . . it has become a well of His love and living water . . . God's love has been shed abroad in our heart . . . by the Holy Spirit . . . and we must begin to draw on it . . . and pour it out over every situation and circumstance . . . and in every relationship . . . allowing HIS love to make the difference. Obviously, our "natural love" falls short . . . but God has made His great love accessible to us . . . through the power of His Spirit . . . but we must make the decision to appropriate and apply it.

John 16:33: I have told you these things so that "in me" you may have peace. In the world "you will have trouble and suffering" . . . but take courage—I have conquered and overcome the world.

"In Him" . . . we will overcome and conquer this world. The key is "in me"!!

When we operate outside of Him . . . and His Word and ways, then we become offended . . . and unable to deal with the problems of the day.

Situations and circumstances of life and people . . . will bring troubles and despair . . . if we forget that His love is always "there."

It "has been" shed abroad in our hearts.
Let's draw on it and apply it liberally
Love lavishly and live abundantly.

CHAPTER 45

Heaven's Hope Chest

Open . . . Heaven's hope chest
Come . . . and look inside
See all the special treasures
I have stored up for my bride

I long to adorn you
With jewels of every hue
I long to open up my coffers
And pour out over you

Heavenly solutions
And answers . . . all you need
Are within my special hope chest
It's filled for your eyes to see

That I am always with you
Right here by your side
And I am pouring out Heaven's riches
As I prepare my bride

Supernatural provision and
Miracles are in my hand
I am leading my beloved
Into the promised land

I'm opening my love chest
As you find your hope in me
It will all turn out the way
That I planned it would be

So no need for you to worry
Just meditate in me
And I will produce the promise
And you'll have eyes to see

That the day is soon appearing
When I will come for you . . . my bride
And I will find you worthy
As you've been tested and tried

In the fires of adversity
And the furnace of my grace
You will stand transparent
Reflecting Heaven's face

Prepared and ready
For our "special day"
My beloved . . .
It's time to come away . . .

Intimacy . . . is the key that unlocks the hope chest of heaven . . .

As you come away into my secret place
All things will be accessible through the administration of my grace,
I so desire for my bride to be blessed
Come away . . . and open Heaven's hope chest . . .

CHAPTER 46

Hope

As I spent time with The Lord today . . . He said to me . . . my people need their HOPE stirred up . . . They "cope" with situations . . . when they have a "hope" for change . . . in me.

So often God encourages me when I feel without hope . . . when I feel like nothing is going to change . . . when I lose hope in people and things . . . He lovingly reveals to me that when I start feeling "hopeless," I make my decisions about things based on what I "see" and reminds me that my hope must not be in "the natural" but rather in His "supernatural ability" to change things when I simply trust Him.

Faith is the "substance" of things HOPED for . . . the "evidence" of things not yet seen.

This is not defining what faith is in totality . . . but rather it shows us what faith "does" . . . in an operative sense. "Faith undergirds" what we "hope" for. Faith and hope are power twins that "work together" exercising patience to receive the promise of God in our lives.

"Substance" means "that which stands under." Faith is the foundation for what we hope for . . . faith is the foundation for our belief in Jesus . . . our relationship with God and everything else that it implies within His purpose. Faith is the very beginning of everything that really matters spiritually in our lives. Without faith we cannot be saved. Without faith it is impossible to please God. Without faith we cannot appropriate any of the promises of God. Without faith . . . we have no real hope.

The hope made available through faith is a "confident expectation" a firm assurance of things uncertain and unknown . . . it should be an enduring virtue of our Christian life. Real love springs from hope (Colossians 1:4-5). Hope produces joy and peace in our lives through the power of the Spirit (Romans 12:12, 15:13). Paul attributes his apostolic calling to the hope of eternal glory (Titus 1:1-2). Our hope in the return of Jesus is our motivation to walk purely before God (Titus 2:11-14, 1 John 3:3).

Hope can never be dependent on peace in our circumstance . . . justice in the world . . . success in our business . . . and righteousness and fairness in the land.

Hope is willing to wait through the situations of life, not being moved by unanswered questions . . . or a future that is unknown . . . or unsure. Hope always sees God's hand in the best and brightest circumstance, as well as in the worst and darkest ones. Hope lives for today . . . expects great things of tomorrow . . . believes that joy will come out of sadness . . . and finds new beginnings in the midst of the old ones . . . We choose to exercise hope in our lives.

Romans 15:13: May the "God of hope" fill you with all joy and peace as you trust in Him, so that you may "overflow with hope" . . . by the power of the Holy Spirit.

Through faith in HIM . . .

Hope is a certainty
It's for now . . . and for sure . . .
Hope brings the answer
When our faith will endure.

Hope for our problems
Hope to regain what was lost
Comes through our faith
But starts with the cross.

The day that He died
He sealed the deal . . .
That our faith and our hope
In Him . . . would be real.

Hope for the future
Through faith in His plan
The two working together
Empowers every woman and man.

To hold fast to the promise
Expecting God to come through
He promised He'd do it . . .
And His Word . . . is true . . .

Ephesians 1:18
I pray that the eyes of your heart may be enlightened in order that you may know the hope to which he has called you . . . the riches of his glorious inheritance in his Holy people . . .

CHAPTER 47

Be a Sermon

So many today want to "talk about" what's happening . . . I want to "see it" in their lives . . . There is too much "talking" and not enough "walking" going on in the lives of "believers" . . . Many arguing and fighting over what is and is not for today . . . like "they" decide . . . how crazy . . . God can do whatever HE wants to do . . . HE IS GOD!

You may be able to argue with my "opinion" but you can't argue my "experience" with God . . . He is a blessing God . . . He delights and takes pleasure in the prosperity of His people . . . When we operate in His Word and principles . . . as our soul prospers so shall we prosper in ALL things.

God's Word is right and true . . . and when we are obedient to do . . . what He tells me and you . . . We shall prosper and be in good health too.

I'd rather "see" a sermon
Than "hear" what you have to say . . .
I'd rather that you "show" me . . .
Not just "tell" me the way . . .

My eyes are better students
More observant than my ears
Messages and methods confuse
But an example's always clear . . .

A true leader is the preacher
Who follows his word with deeds . . .
To see his faith "in action"
Is what the people need

Others will learn to walk it out
If they can "watch and do"
When they see our life transparent
They'll know our word is true . . .

The sermons we deliver
May be anointed and sound
But words alone will never
Turn a life around . . .

They may not comprehend
All the scriptures that we give . . .
But there's no misunderstanding
All the scriptures that we "live"

People hear . . . what they "see" . . . much more than what "is said"

Matthew 6:33
Seek "first the Kingdom of Heaven" and "HIS righteousness" and "ALL" these "things" SHALL be added to you!

Seek the Kingdom of God above all else, and live righteously, and He will give you "everything you need."

Proverbs 8:18 With me are riches and honor, enduring wealth and prosperity.

Psalm 35:27 . . . Let them shout for joy . . . and be glad, those that favour "my righteous cause" . . . and let them say continually . . . Let the LORD be magnified, who has pleasure in the "prosperity of his servant."

God is pleased when we walk in His abundant supply . . . He IS Jehovah Jireh our provider . . . He is a great Father and does not want to see his children begging bread and not amply provided for ... He set out a blueprint for success for us in His Word and as we endeavour to be "Doers" of it ... we shall benefit from the blessings of it.

Deuteronomy 29:9 ... Carefully follow the "terms of this covenant" so that "you may prosper in everything you do."

Argue as you will with me ... His Word makes it very clear ... it's not about "money" it's about "principle" and " prosperity" ... His Word is TRUE and will be established in the lives of those who adhere to it ... meditate upon it and purpose to DO IT!

James 1:22 ... Do not merely listen to the word, and so "deceive" yourselves. DO what it says.

When we purpose in our lives to follow Him in word and deed ... then we become examples of His manifold blessings ... HE IS a blessing God ... and He blesses US that we would be a blessing to others ... He has given us the "treasure" of His Word that we might chart the course of our lives and be successful ... prosperous ... effective and fruitful. He desires that we would have "more than enough" ... to give into every good work ... and bless those who are less fortunate and in need.

The church is called to lead ... called to have influence and to "impact" the community ... When we will WALK it out ... instead of "talk" about ... We will "be the church" ... a living ... breathing entity ... changing lives ... transforming Cities and shifting Nations for the Glory of God!

Let's not make excuses ... A person who buys his own excuse ... usually attempts to sell it to others.

Let's live without excuse ... and live out the Word ... The Word ... WORKS! It shall not return void ... it shall accomplish whatever it is sent to do ... and HE himself watches over HIS word to perform it! Praise God!!

CHAPTER 48

Choosing Honesty

The single most important element in our relationships, is real honesty. Honesty with God, with ourselves and with others. Jesus called it "walking in the light."

We all make mistakes, exercise poor judgment and can operate in less than appropriate behaviour from time to time. We just need to humble ourselves and deal with it. No one ever choked to death by swallowing their pride . . .

The quality of our life is much more determined in our responses to the things that happen, then in what actually happens. Life happens, good and bad, happy and sad in the great times and through the pain, a rainbow appears with both sun and rain!

Let us not "be hurt" or "hurt others" by any selfish deed, thoughtless word, or act of disunity, deception or untruth. May we never pass by without seeing a true need or may we never sin by sitting in silence when we should rise up defend and speak the truth.

The right choice is never usually the easy choice. The easy choice is usually the wrong choice . . . and no choice . . . is still a choice . . . Making our own choice takes away the opportunity of blaming someone else for the way things turned out . . . We need to see the long term consequences of our own choices and our decision to put "our will" above God's will . . .

It's the choices we make that show what we are made of . . . our true nature and character. Abilities, gifts and talents have nothing to do character. The fruit of our character is evident in the choices we make. Our character is forged in the fire of choosing to do the right thing, answer the right way, live the right way, choosing truth over lies and making a decision to be "on God's side."

There is no problem we cannot resolve and overcome unless we choose not to. Our inability to say we're sorry, reconcile and restore is evidence of the wrong spirit in operation in our lives. We isolate and re-locate instead of negotiate and set it straight when we refuse to deal with issues in our lives. Sooner or later it re-visits us. With God we just keep taking the test . . . till we pass it.

God desires for us to be fruitful and for the fruit of our lives to feed others. If we are honest with ourselves, would people come back for more after they tasted of our fruit? When the Holy Spirit controls our lives, He will produce this kind of fruit in us, love, joy, peace, patience, kindness, goodness, faithfulness, gentleness and self-control. When we are in control we will get a much different result . . . If we plant Crab Apple seeds we will never get Honey Crisps . . .

The lack of integrity for a moment can undo the work of a whole life time . . . In the end . . . our choices determine who we really are. Our life is a matter of choice not chance. Unfortunately, for most of us, changing is what we choose to do when we have no options left . . . Thank God for HIS continual goodness and that His mercies are new every morning!!

CHAPTER 49

Not Living the Lie

I've known people who were fanatical about dressing modestly . . . being on time for their church commitments and "looking good" . . . yet they think nothing of manipulating a situation by using untruths. Spouses lie to one another in the name of "keeping the peace," parents lie to their own children and vice versa. Advertisers lie to sell products. Politicians lie in order to spin things their own way, lawyers lie to protect the guilty, people lie about their taxes; lies, lies, lies . . .

A store manager heard his clerk tell a customer, "No, ma'am, we haven't had any for a while, and it doesn't look as if we'll be getting any soon." Horrified, the manager came running over to the customer and said, "Of course we'll have some soon. We placed an order last week." Then the manager drew the clerk aside. "Never," he snarled, "Never, never, never say we're out of anything" . . . say "we've got it on order" and "it's coming soon." "Now, what was it she wanted anyway?" The clerk said, "Rain!"

We say that honesty is the best policy . . . and honesty pays . . . but actually often times it costs . . .

Doing right is its own reward . . . Proverbs 12:22 says . . . Lying lips are abomination to the LORD: but they that deal truly are his delight.

You can fool some people and be a secret servant of fraud . . .

You can hide your lies . . . but you can't fool God!

Psalms 101:5—Whoso "privily" slanders his neighbour . . . in a "secret way" behind their back . . . (with the intention of doing harm to another's reputation) him will I cut off . . .

I like this story about the man who spread lies about his Pastor . . . after a time he was convicted . . . he came to his Pastor and repented . . . asking him how he could make it right. The pastor told him to get some feather pillows and rip them open, and place one feather on every porch in their community. This seemed strange, but he did what he was told. He went back to the Pastor and said he was finished to which the Pastor responded . . . now go back and pick them all up . . . The bewildered man said but how can I? The wind has taken them who knows where.

The Pastor said, "So it is with the words you have spoken about me." . . .

We can repent and we can be forgiven . . . but there are long reaching consequences to the sin of lying.

Colossians 3:9-10 . . . Do not lie to one another, seeing that you have put off the old self with its practices and have "put on the new self" which is "being renewed" in knowledge after the image of its creator.

To thine own self be TRUE. Are you known to be a truly honest person, or do people have to question you and wonder about your genuineness. Do you have a reputation as a person who speaks truth or spreads rumours and slanders and engages in Godless chatter . . . Is your word as good as your signature . . . Do you do what you say you will do . . . and above ALL do you tell the truth even when it will cost you something . . .

CHAPTER 50

Being Like Him

Our character is being proven as we go through the tests and trials of life . . . and we get to the other side of the experience we give glory to God for the changes it has wrought in us . . .

Untried . . . untested . . . untempered faith is not overcoming faith . . . it's fair weather faith . . . When we will "exercise our faith" through the hard times we will be refined and purified and become more like precious silver and gold . . . more like God . . . but when we allow our flesh and our emotions to determine the outcome we become hard hearted to the ways of God and we become like a clanging cymbal.

No one ever choked to death swallowing their pride . . . but many dreams have died and many a call has gone by the wayside . . . and many have lost a great deal . . . from the bitterness and unforgiveness they sustain from chewing on old wounds . . . grievances and offences.

We are called and commanded to forgive each other . . . if we expect that God will forgive us. The Bible makes this very clear . . . Jesus himself said . . . that if you do not forgive your brother when he trespasses against you . . . neither will I forgive you . . . You can't make that say something else . . . It is VERY clear. We cannot hold on to past issues and history if we want to move forward and be a new "history maker."

It's time to let go of the old
and take hold of the new . . .
God is beckoning me and you . . .

Forgive and forget
Like God does for you
If you expect to be forgiven
For the things you do . . .

Yesterday's old wounds
Will never be gone . . .
If we hold fast to them . . .
Instead of moving on . . .

It's time to move on . . .
Time to move up . . . and in . . .
We have the victory . . .
But we have to choose to win . . .

It is always our decision . . .
What we will and will not do . . .
We can say NO to the things
God wants from me and you . . .

We can choose our own way
And run our own race . . .
But when we obey His Word
There's power in "our" place

Through the good times and the bad ones
Through each and every test
He strengthens our faith
And causes us to be blessed . . .

All the things we go through
Every trouble and care . . .
Only proves the steadfast truth
God is always there

He's walking through it with us
Giving encouragement and grace

As He refines us in his fire
Till we reflect His face . . .

Our faith becomes perfected
When we will just press in . . .
Trusting God no matter what
And being made "more like Him."

Our destiny is to be made into the likeness and image of Jesus . . . and whatever we do "for Him" will flow out of that place of being like Him . . . It is "in Him" . . . that we move and breathe and have "our being."

CHAPTER 51

As a Man Thinks in His Heart

As a man thinks in his heart . . . so is the man. We will never "feel" the way we want to . . . until we "think" the way we ought to.

Would we really rather hate . . . be estranged . . . and be right, than be reconciled and be at peace with God, ourselves and others? Unforgiveness is a land mine in the path of a believer . . .

Anger and unforgiveness are the ugly stepdaughters of offence . . .

The spirit of unforgiveness still looms large in the body of Christ . . . When we are unforgiving . . . we are demanding perfection from others . . . and a level of conduct that we ourselves cannot obtain or maintain. When we choose to withhold forgiveness we must be prepared to reap according to the measure we have sown. God will not be mocked . . . for whatsoever a man shall sow . . . so shall that man also reap!!

Our failure to forgive proves to be a devastating form of self-punishment and a destructive "land-mine" that hinders the walking out of our faith . . .

In Ephesians 4:32 the apostle Paul writes, "Be kind to one another, tender-hearted, forgiving each other, just as God in Christ also has forgiven you."

This is not always easy when someone has committed a terrible offence against us . . . and sometimes it is not easy when someone has committed a small offence that we have exaggerated and harbored through seasons of our lives . . .

The enemy will entice us to be "angry" . . . demanding an apology . . . demanding retribution . . . demanding that "our feelings" be validated and considered, convincing us that we had it harder than we really did . . . embellishing and amplifying the "real" truth.

Unforgiveness ... is a "deliberate mindset" to resent both the wrong that was done and the wrongdoer ... and to seek revenge ... through retaliation ... or through loss of relationship ... as we punish others by "our bad behaviour" towards them ...

In Ephesians 4:31 Paul associates unforgiveness with bitterness, wrath, anger, clamor, slander, and malice.

It is hard to understand why we would choose these "painful attitudes" over expressing tenderness, gentleness, and a forgiving spirit.

Many people are physically ill today because they do just that. They live day by day ... year by year ... with "disease" and the cancer of an unforgiving heart ... silently and slowly taking their own life ...

As mature believers ... we must be aware of the enemy's tactics and choose the peace of the path to forgiveness as we walk in love and faith into the plan of God for our lives ...

We have a great capacity to look at others through magnifying glasses while we look at ourselves through rose coloured ones.

Every story has two sides and a truth that resides somewhere in the middle. The problem with us wanting to be "dead right" is ... it's usually at the expense of killing relationship.

An unforgiving heart ... clings to the past ... refusing to let go of old offences ... continuing to judge behaviours of others ... and rehearsing old experiences ... An unforgiving heart also refuses to extend to others what our Heavenly Father has extended to us.

In Ephesians 4:32 the apostle insists upon our "forgiving each other ... just as God in Christ also has forgiven you." IF you do not forgive others neither will I forgive you.

Matthew 6:14-15 For if you forgive others their trespasses, your Heavenly Father will also forgive you, but "if you do not forgive others" their trespasses, neither will your Father forgive your trespasses. That's pretty serious!!!

If we continue to act with a resentful . . . unyielding attitude . . . we will have to continually deal with negative consequences in our life. When bitterness takes root in our heart . . . it spreads its poison to choke out every other Godly trait that abides there . . . When we "choose" to be unforgiving . . . we make a deliberate decision and we cause our own self-inflicted pain . . . We carry "the illusion" that other people are responsible because they caused our trouble . . . our misery . . . our addiction . . . our life style . . . but in reality . . . "we have chosen" to take on this form of self-imposed bondage . . . by our own decisions. We have opened the door to the devil with our own behaviour and then refused to do what we needed to do to close it.

We will have trouble standing before God and "blaming" someone else for our own bad attitudes . . . choices and decisions.

Our refusal to forgive is a selfish act of pride and rebellion . . . and it is a deliberate act of disobedience to the Word of God . . . that we will be accountable for.

Our witness . . . and our overall spiritual growth are terribly weakened by a heart that carries bitterness . . . resentment and unforgiveness. Every other aspect of our life will be affected . . . when we are loaded down with the stress and anxiety . . . of holding on to the darkness and its deeds when God has translated us into His marvelous light.

No one enjoys being around bitter people . . . so poisoned by the "past" that they are dead to the future God has for them . . . We will never "move on" if the desire to "hold on" is greater . . . We must choose . . . It's up to us if we WIN . . . or LOSE!

Philippians 3:13—Brothers . . . not that I count myself to have apprehended: BUT this "one thing I DO" . . . FORGETTING those things which are behind . . . and reaching forward to those things which are before . . . to the "High Call" that is in Christ Jesus!!

CHAPTER 52

Casting Off the Works of the Darkness

Romans 13:12-14
The night is far spent, the day is at hand. Therefore let us "cast off the works of darkness" . . . and let us "put on the armor of light" . . . Let us "walk properly" as in the day . . . not in revelry and drunkenness, not in lewdness and lust, not in "strife and envy" . . . But "put on the Lord Jesus Christ" . . . and make "no provision for the flesh" . . . to fulfill its lusts.

This scripture warns us about not giving into our flesh . . . and allowing the devil to take us out of the place of blessing . . . Many "branches" have broken "themselves free" of the vine . . . and will soon feel the drought . . . God is the one who calls and positions us to ministries and church families and fellowships . . . and when we become offended and take ourselves out from under cover we are prey for the enemy . . . and he will work until he steals our faith kills our vision and destroys our lives. The predator will always take out those who are estranged from the flock . . . and cause barrenness to come upon them.

The Word of The Lord today said that in the next three years we will see the vision double in size . . . and provision for the vision and financial stability will take hold . . . God is causing the fullness of the vision to become manifest . . .

Many livelihoods and destinies will come forth out of the creative flow of ministry as we begin to infiltrate the mountains of society . . . family . . . arts and entertainment . . . business . . . media . . . education . . . government and religion. It's time for our light to be seen, and our voice to be heard.

The Lord has a harvest field set aside and is taking many into His refining fire even now . . . remember . . . as steel goes through the fire . . . it becomes stronger and stronger . . . and as silver is refined it reflects, the face of the silversmith.

So just press into the refiner's fire a little longer . . . knowing that it's always the "hottest" before the harvest . . .

Many have grown weary in well doing and have stepped out of the fires of adversity and have not yielded to the refining process . . . they have stepped out of unity . . . with the body and the family of believers God has placed them in . . . The enemy is causing people to advocate their place . . . becoming offended and causing offence . . . We are called to "take ground" not "give it up" . . .

Many people have walked away . . . walked out of their place . . . the devil talked them into giving up and giving in . . . letting go and allowing their flesh and emotions to rule . . . and win . . .

We must guard our heart . . . A falling away has already occurred because many have not guarded their heart and have allowed themselves to become hard hearted . . . prideful and resistant . . . Be aware . . . as you move and transition into the deeper things of God . . . the enemy will oppose you and work at taking you out . . . Many have fallen prey to the bait of satan . . . The devil uses every trick in the book to keep us from pressing in . . . because it works . . .

Our "flesh" is an easy target for the enemy when we do not take authority over it and make it come in line with our spirit!! . . . We "choose" to crucify our flesh . . . by "allowing our spirit" to lead the way . . . When flesh becomes the leader . . . our senses say "retreat" . . . and we operate in disobedience and we suffer defeat!

Our "ability" to come into unity speaks of our "maturity" as a Christian. We are not called to stir up things with our brothers and sisters . . . or be the devil's advocate . . . We are called of God to bring unity! We are called to resolve conflict . . . not cause it . . . We should never be "hard to work with." We are called to be easy to be entreated . . .

Unity is a choice . . . and so is disunity . . . When we bring disunity . . . it did not come from the heart of God . . . We must choose to deny self . . . defeat our own flesh . . . and chose to NOT sow seeds of discord . . . Unity is the key to blessing!

If we cannot defeat self we can't defeat anything . . . we must win the battle from the inside out . . . We have to give up our right to "be right."

Disunity is rooted in pride . . . There is nothing that will keep us from the fullness of God's best like pride . . . it is our enemy and God's enemy . . . Pride . . . turned an angel into a devil.

We are called to love those that are not easy to love . . . Unity is a choice . . . We always have a choice . . . and the choice we exercise . . . reveals "our" heart.

There is always a remnant in God ready to catch the wave of blessing that's on the way . . . those who are faithful and positioned to receive from the Spirit . . . Our faith works by love . . . and we must "choose" to operate in love if we expect our faith to access the promise of God. This is the season when the remnant will be revealed . . . where our priorities will be laid bare . . . and the fruit of our choices will be evidenced.

This is a pivotal time:

God is putting things in place . . .
And He is picking up the pace . . .
He is rightly aligning and preparing . . .
Those called to fulfill His Kingdom plan . . .
Those who are given over and saying
Yes Lord . . . I will and I can . . .
Those pressing into His purpose . . .
His vision and His way . . .
Those stepping up and stepping in
To a brand new day . . .

The season is upon us for high impact . . . A great and effectual door has been opened and God has made us ready to enter in . . . and Win!!

CHAPTER 53

Take the High Road

As we were driving today through Pottstown PA today, I saw this sign . . . "The best way to not get stuck in the mud . . . is to take the high road" . . . It just jumped out at me and I couldn't get it out of my mind.

When I got back to our room I began to ask The Lord about it. I believe that God speaks to us through all things if we will listen and inquire of Him. He began to share with me that many who lived in this area were snared by their "own choices" . . . that they were leaning on their own understanding . . . and they were not acknowledging and asking Him about the matters in their lives. He said they actually took "pride" in the fact that they are free to choose for themselves . . . and they are . . . but they are also "NOT FREE" from the consequences of their choice . . . and many are being ravished over and over by the consequences of poor choices . . .

God has given us a free will. He has given us the right to choose. As believers, He has an expectation of us to operate in the safety of His Word. The Bible says that IF we love Him . . . We will "obey" Him. If we will acknowledge Him in ALL our ways . . . He will direct our path . . . When we will "walk" in His Word we will walk the life of blessing and success . . . It won't always be an easy walk . . . there will be a few hills and valley . . . a few bumps and turns but our destination will be sure. A good Father in the natural always wants His children to be safe and successful . . . how much more our Heavenly Father . . .

Proverbs 3:5-6 Trust in the Lord with all your heart, and lean not in your own understanding . . . in all your ways "submit" to Him . . . and He will direct your path and make it straight . . .

He has given us the right to choose . . . but when we will "submit" that right back to Him . . . He will help us win, not lose . . .

It's up to us to choose
The way we're going to go
Will we take the high road
Or settle for the low . . .

In life . . . we must make decisions
We have the right to choose
Some will lead to victory
And some will make us lose.

Circumstance may try to guide us
Down a dark and troubled way
But God has given us free will
To choose our path today

When we make decisions
We exercise the right to choose
But we alone will pay the price
When a wrong choice will make us lose

"Many" travel on the low road
With all its troubles and concerns
Never willing to make the change
Never willing to take the turns

God is on the "high road"
Above the mud and mire below
On the "highway of holiness"
That's the way we're called to go

We can face what life delivers
And stay steadfast and strong . . .
And trust that God will lead us
When we're on the road where we belong

Taking the high road
Is a brave and heroic feat
The "narrow way" to life
Is not called "easy street"

It's the road . . . less travelled
The path of challenges and tests
But it's the road where Jesus walks
And the way where we'll be blessed . . .

It leads us to God's perfect place . . .
And away from selfish destinations
It's the road under construction
Where we "work out" our salvation

It's always our decision
What you will and will not do
But God is standing on the road
And He is waiting there for me and you

He's given us a free will . . .
But we can't act like we don't know . . .
That it is always up to you and me . . .
To take the high road or the low . . .

Isaiah 35:8-11 A highway shall be there, and a road ... And it shall be called the Highway of Holiness ... The unclean shall not pass over it ... But it shall be for others ... Whoever walks the road, although a fool ... Shall not go astray ... No lion shall be there ... Nor shall any ravenous beast go up on it ... It shall not be found there ... But the redeemed shall walk there ... And the ransomed of the Lord shall return ... And come to Zion with singing ... With everlasting joy on their heads ... They shall obtain joy and gladness ... And sorrow and sighing shall flee away.

CHAPTER 54

Be Made More Like Him

John 1:12 . . . to all those who did receive Him . . . to those who believed in His name . . .
He "gave the right" to become children of God . . .

We have been "given the right" to become the sons and daughters, the children of
God. We exercise that right by exercising behaviour worthy of His name. Everything
we do is a self portrait of "who" we are. Let's autograph our work with the excellence
of Spirit our Father has placed within us, and let "what we do" evidence that we are
becoming more "like Him" This is the season we are in . . . the becoming more like
Him . . . season.

When we spend the time it takes in the secret place . . . signs and wonders and
miracles will be the result. Personal change . . . healing and wholeness will be the
outcome . . . of setting ourselves apart in His presence . . . As our soul prospers . . .
so shall we prosper in ALL things . . . character . . . integrity . . . honesty . . . loyalty
and financially . . . as we are conditioned by His heart to desire to "give" into "every
good work" . . . according to His purposes. True godly prosperity is a gift to us from
our Father . . .

Jesus told those who followed him . . . that if they had seen him . . . they had also
seen His Father . . . I pray today that as people look at me . . . it would be . . . his love
and grace they'd see . . . that all that I say and all that I do . . . would point others
Lord to you . . .

May I be made into your image and likeness
More and more each day
That I would be prepared and willing
To follow you in every way . . .

To allow change and transformation
To have . . . its perfect work in me . . .
That I would be an example
That others could truly "see"

For eyes are better students
More observant than ears
Messages and methods confuse
But an example's always clear . . .

Lord let me be a person
Who is faithful my word to do . . .
Remembering always
To thine own self I must be true

Yielding to your Spirit
As you perfect in me your plan
That I would be filled with true desire
To be a God . . . woman!!

Step right up and in . . . to this season of being made "more like Him."

CHAPTER 55

Don't Personalize Your Problem

Did you ever listen to some people who, when they are suffering from an infirmity ... say things like "my illness" ... "my migraine" ... "my injuries." They "personalize" the ailment and experience ... instead of seeing it as an attack from the devil ... God is NOT the author of sickness and death and disease ...

He is the author of healing and life!

God's Word is our remedy ... it is a medicine ... and a cure ... and as we meditate and ponder on the truth of His Word ... we will appropriate and embrace and receive all that was purchased for us at the cross ...

When we begin to realize who we are ... and who it is that lives on the inside of us ... then we will walk in the truth ... that "by His stripes ... we are healed" that we are not waiting on healing ... it was already purchased for us ... We just need to appropriate it.

Isaiah 53:4-9 ... Surely He took of our infirmities ... and carried our sorrows ... Yet we considered Him ... stricken by God ... smitten by Him and afflicted ... He was pierced for our transgressions ... he was bruised for our iniquities ... the punishment that brought us peace ... was upon Him ... and by His wounds we ARE healed!!

"Unbelieving Christians" do exist and they try to discredit the power of the Holy Spirit moving in our lives now ... and the "present day ministry of Jesus" flowing through those who believe and follow Him ... in the working of miracles, signs and wonders ... but they can NEVER discredit the work that was already accomplished at the cross!

We appropriated and received salvation by "confessing with our mouth" that Jesus is Lord ... and "believing in our heart" that God raised him from the dead ...

God's Word in our mouth is just as powerful as God's Word in God's mouth . . . because the power is in the "Word" . . . "It will not return void" it WILL accomplish whatever it is sent to do . . . God himself "watches over" His Word to "perform it" . . . We need to "believe it" and "speak it"

For it is with our heart we believe and are justified . . . and it is with our mouth that we confess and are saved . . .

Salvation is the beginning of our relationship and journey with God . . . It is a daily walk in His presence . . . growing in His Word and His plan and purpose for our life . . . Paul told us to work out our salvation with fear and trembling . . . purposely laying down our own desires . . . dying to self daily and making a decision to walk in ALL of His ways . . . It is a process of continual change and transformation . . .

We appropriate and receive healing in the same way . . . by "confessing with our mouth" that our healing was already purchased . . . and by "believing in our heart" that by His wounds . . . we are healed . . .

As we "meditate" and "medicate" in God's healing words . . . we till and cultivate the soil of our heart until it is prepared and ready to accept the seeds of His truth . . . and bring forth a harvest of well being . . . healing and wholeness . . . into our lives . . .

We believe we receive "when we pray" and we stand in faith as it manifests in the natural realm . . . although "behold all things are new" happened in the spirit the day we were saved . . . everything in the natural did not change immediately, but by faith we believe that we are a work in progress and He is faithful to finish the work he began . . . Salvation was His plan . . .

Everything may not change immediately in the realm of healing in the natural but we still believe we receive "when we pray" and God is faithful to finish the work He began . . . Healing was His plan . . .

Jeremiah 17:14 "Heal me, O LORD . . . and I shall be healed . . . save me . . . and I shall be saved for you are my praise."

Once we finally understand that healing is as much a part of the finished work of grace as salvation is . . . and that it was paid for at the same time with the same healing Blood . . . we will faithfully confess . . . "You did it for me Lord . . . and I will agree with your Word and believe and confess that I have healing . . . just as I have salvation . . . and it's mine NOW . . . in Jesus name" . . .

CHAPTER 56

No Matter What – God IS

I heard The Lord say . . .

Your past does not determine your future . . . your covenant with me does . . .

I can take the "very worst" . . . and bring forth the "very best" . . .

The devil is always speaking lies
To steal your self esteem . . .
Trying to get you out of place . . .
And off of Heaven's team . . .

He plans to steal your faith
And your identity . . .
But whatever you think about yourself
That's what you'll believe

The devil can NEVER stop the plan of God in our lives but WE can . . . IF we decide to agree with the lies of the enemy . . . we will not succeed . . . But when we choose to walk in God's Word . . . actively participating in that which we have heard . . . We will have good success and we will prosper in all our ways . . . as we follow after the plan of God . . . day after day after day . . .

The devil may be able to hinder us . . .
or cause a detour on the road to success
But there will never be a dead end . . .
and God will "always" bless . . .

As we continue to move forward
in His will and in His way . . .

He will fight our battles
And keep the enemy at bay

His grace is sufficient
For everything we need
When we keep our eyes on Jesus
And let His Spirit lead . . .

The Lord says . . .

The past can never dictate
Your future in me . . . it was pre-planned . . .
I never leave you or forsake you . . .
Every moment of your life . . . is in my hand

I knew you in eternity past
I knit you together in the womb
I'm with you in your times of joy
And in your times of gloom . . .

I am always for you
I'm right here . . . on the inside
Perfecting and positioning
My pure and spotless bride . . .

So there's no need for you to worry . . .
Meditate . . . don't fret
The very best is still to come
You've not seen nothing yet!!!!

CHAPTER 57

Loving What God Loves

We must love what God loves . . . and hate what He hates . . .

He loves a cheerful giver . . . He loves justice . . . He loves the righteous . . . he loves those who obey His commands . . . He loves those who pursue Godliness . . . He loves those who fear Him . . .

He hates . . . a proud look . . . He hates a lying tongue . . . He hates hands that shed innocent blood . . . He hates a heart that devises wicked plans . . . He hates feet that are swift in running to evil . . . He hates a false witness who speaks lies . . . He hates the one who sows discord among the brethren . . .

We live in the days of itching ears . . . the feel good Gospel . . . and hyper grace . . . The days where darkness covers the earth . . . and gross darkness the people . . .

Today many have made a "graven image" of God . . . a God that is acceptable to us . . . one we are "willing" to serve . . . A "loving" God . . . who overlooks our sin and doesn't require us to repent and confess any longer . . . A God who no longer has or exercises "righteous anger" . . . A God suitable and satisfactory for us . . . One who is admissible . . . agreeable . . . and reasonable . . . A God who no longer requires us to sacrifice . . . consecrate or set ourselves apart . . .

We have made for ourselves a God . . . who understands that we are too busy . . . too tired . . . too overworked . . . too pre-occupied . . .

The Bible says . . . 'Love the Lord your God with all your heart and with all your soul and with all your strength and with all your mind'; and, 'Love your neighbor as yourself.' That takes energy and purpose . . .

But come on . . .

I have kids to raise . . . and a job to do . . . a house to look after . . . and grass to mow too . . . I've got laundry to wash . . . and groceries to buy . . . I'll see God on Sunday . . . or at least I'll "try" . . . I'm too busy for others . . . not enough hours in the day . . . No time for prayer . . . but I'm doing OK . . . No time for a get away to the secret place . . . but that doesn't matter . . . I can just "call on" His "grace."

I don't make enough money . . . to give to The Lord . . . but He understands that I can't afford . . . to support what He's doing . . . His plans and his way . . . He understands that I have . . . "such a small pay" . . . I have obligations to meet . . . and a house to pay for . . . He knows that I'd give . . . if I only had more . . . My God doesn't require His commands be obeyed . . . I mean . . . I'm in the new . . . the old has passed away . . . There's freedom to give . . . what I "feel" to do . . . I'm under grace . . . the law no longer stands true . . . grace gives me the right to do . . . what I want to . . .

My God "is love" . . . My God is great . . . always accepting . . . My God "doesn't hate" . . . His grace is sufficient to "cover my sin." I tell that to my neighbours while I sip my tonic and gin . . . I can do what I want . . . what makes me feel good . . . it's Ok if I don't . . . though I know that I should . . . God will forgive me . . . I'm just human you see . . . God has no real expectations of me . . . He is all loving . . . He will always forgive . . . it's fine with my God . . . if I live and let live . . .

My God . . . is acceptable . . . tolerant and fair . . . He understands . . . when I'm just not there . . . He's reasonable and agreeable . . . discerning my heart . . . realizing I'm so busy . . . I just can't take part . . . He's admissible and permissive allowing for my slack . . . always waiting patiently for me to get back on track . . . He understands when I'm offended . . . hurt or mad . . . He feels for me when I'm down and sad . . . He made me human . . . He made me this way . . . My God loves me . . . come what may . . .

My God "tolerates" my bad behaviour . . . He doesn't notice when I lie . . . He knows I didn't really mean it . . . I'm really a good guy . . . He overlooks my "opinions" . . .

my emotions and attitude . . . He knows my heart . . . He knows I'm nice . . . though
sometimes I am rude . . .

My God is my comforter . . . he comes along side . . . He is always wooing me . . . to
come and to abide . . . He is always for me . . . no matter what I do . . . it doesn't really
matter . . . what I put others through . . . cause I know . . . I'm his favourite . . . I'm
his pure and spotless bride . . . it doesn't matter to "My Father" . . . that I cheated
and I lied . . .

My God is ever gracious . . . forbearing . . . and true . . . He always loves His children . . . no matter what they do . . . His grace . . . it is sufficient . . . to cover all our
mess . . . but only when we repent . . . and are willing to confess . . . We must always
do our best . . . to turn from wrong to right . . . always living in His truth . . . and walking in His light . . . My God . . . he paid the total price . . . on that dark and dreadful
day . . . He laid down his life . . . and took my sin . . . to make for me a way . . . To live
my life for Jesus . . . and die to that "old man." He filled me with His Spirit . . . so He
knows I can . . . Live a life that's free from sin . . . by faith and through His grace . . .
I'm an overcomer . . . who reflects my saviour's face . . .

But only when I "choose" to . . . can I walk it out . . . only when I move by faith not
entertaining doubt . . . and only when I'm willing . . . to confess my sin . . . can I be
forgiven . . . turn and come back in . . . God's Word hasn't changed . . . no matter
what some say . . . He's the same forever . . . today and yesterday . . .

Let's not be deceived . . . by the doctrines of devils in this hour . . . His Word is still
the truth and it carries all of heaven's power . . . Yes His grace . . . stands forever . . .
and His Word is true and right . . . Repent . . . confess . . . turn once again . . . and be
"pleasing in His sight" . . .

I'm looking for the one . . . who gives me her life . . . I'm looking for a bride . . . not
a common law wife . . . one who is sold out . . . fully fashioned in me . . . I'm looking
beloved for intimacy . . . not looking for someone with so much to do . . . looking for
love . . . that is faithful and true . . . with all of your heart and soul and mind . . . yes

this is the love . . . this is the kind . . . the love that is poured out lavishly . . . in the place of intimacy . . . I will fully know you . . . and you will fully know me . . . You will tell me all your secrets . . . your troubles and plight . . . and by the power of my Spirit . . . you will rise up and fight . . . and you will be refined in the furnace of my grace . . . and others will see "me" when they look on your face . . .

I'm looking to be first . . . in your plans for the day . . . as you walk in my truth . . . my light and my way . . . Not looking to be left out . . . passed over or missed . . . I'm looking to be on your favourites list . . .

Your life will tell "my story" and all that I have done . . . when you spend some more time basking in the glorious Son . . .

Confession is an admission of weakness and at the same time a sign of real strength of character.

Prove by the way you live that you have really turned from your sins and turned to God . . . Matthew 3:8 . . . NLT

1 John 1:9 . . . If we confess our sins, he is faithful and just and will forgive us our sins and purify us from all unrighteousness.

He who conceals his sins does not prosper . . . but whoever confesses and renounces them finds mercy . . . Proverbs 28:13

Repentance means I leave the sin
That I so loved before . . .
And "show" that I am grieved by it
By "doing it" NO more . . .

CHAPTER 58

Psalm 101

When David penned this Psalm . . . it was written in the genuine spirit of a man after God's own heart . . . it is a solemn vow which he made to God when he took upon himself the charge of a family and the kingdom.

Whether it was penned when he entered into his governmental call immediately after the death of Saul (as some think), or when he began to reign over all Israel . . . and brought up the ark to the city of David (as others think) . . . it is an excellent plan and model for good government . . . for our personal good moral behaviour . . . and is applicable to our personal families . . . and church families as well . . .

It is the Psalm of the "household" and instructs all that are in any sphere of authority . . . whether larger or small to use their power so as to make it a terror to evildoers . . . and a praise to those that do well and conduct themselves in the love and truth of God's instruction . . .

David's vow was that he would detest and disapprove of all manner of wickedness . . . and that he would favour and encourage such as were virtuous and following after truth and mercy . . .

David felt he must govern . . . in the justice of God . . . and be one who loves righteousness and hates wickedness . . . This psalm shows us that those who lead . . . in families . . . church and government . . . should teach, and admonish, and engage themselves and one another in walking in the righteousness of God . . . that peace may be upon them and that "HIS" presence would be with them.

I will sing of our love and justice
I will before you stand and praise . . .
I will walk Lord before you blameless
Before you my life . . . I'll raise

175

I will walk within my house
With a heart blameless . . . and true
I will set my eyes on you . . . Lord
And nothing evil will I do . . .

The deeds of the darkness
Will have no place in me . . .
Those who do not serve you
With them . . . I will not be . . .

Those who slander others in secret
I will not ignore and tolerate
But I will speak . . . and bring your justice
Proud hearts and haughty eyes . . . you hate . . .

Let me be established with the faithful
That they may dwell with me
Those given over to your goodness
Moving in the fullness of your ministry

No one practicing deceit
Speaking falsely . . . and bringing disdain
But those living in the truth
They will rule and reign . . .

For there is a silencing coming
Of those who do wicked in the land
Those who lie and bear false witness
With those . . . I will not stand.

The shaking in the earth is still upon us in this hour . . . for the fear of The Lord shall be re-established in the House of God . . . No matter how many times we try in our human desire to make God more permissible . . . more tolerant and admissible . . . He is still justice . . . and righteousness and truth . . . and Judgement still begins in The House of The Lord . . . The day is coming and will soon be upon us that we will have to stand up for what we say we believe . . . Many hide in the shadows and utter words against God and His precepts . . . Time for His people to "walk and talk" the truth . . .

1 Peter 4:17

For it is time for judgment to begin with God's household . . . and if it begins with us . . . what will the outcome be for those who do not obey the gospel of God?

CHAPTER 59

Proverbs 4:20–26

Proverbs 4:20-26

My son, pay attention to what I say . . . turn your ear to my words. Do not let them out of your sight . . . keep them within your heart . . . for they are life to those who find them and health to one's whole body.

Above all else, guard your heart . . . for everything you do flows from it. Keep your mouth free of perversity . . . keep corrupt talk far from your lips . . . Let your eyes look straight ahead . . . fix your gaze directly before you . . . Give careful thought to the paths for your feet . . . and be steadfast in all your ways.

Wisdom is the principle thing
Thus saith The Lord
But above "ALL" else guard your heart
"Offence" . . . you can't afford . . .

From your heart all things will flow
So be mindful of what you speak
Don't press into what is evil
Watch your mouth and watch your feet

Offence will take us "out of place"
It's the devils tool . . . and snare . . .
It causes us to turn away
And no longer really care . . .

So many think they have God's love
But you can tell what's at the core . . .
When you really want to "work it out"
And they . . . "walk out" the door . . .

God is testing motives
He's weighing the intentions of our hearts
Are we lifting up the shield of faith
Or shooting fiery darts . . .

Are we walking in his love and plan . . .
Or allowing "flesh" to lead the way
Are we representing Jesus
In all we do and say . . .

Do we manipulate in silence
Stubborn and unwilling to budge
Does our pride and self importance
Make us arbitrate and judge . . .

When we are truly "born again"
The old man must pass away
With all his "old actions" put to rest
And all the "old things" he has to say . . .

For we are no longer that person
Who gossips and complains . . .
That "old man" is dead and gone
When we've been "born again"

No longer do we steal or lie
We don't cheat and fool around
We've been purchased by His blood
And He has turned our life around . . .

No longer are we lost . . .
And burdened with our sin . . .

Jesus came and paid the price
So you and I could win . . .

He poured out His life and blood
Covered our sin with love and grace
He came so we could be "reborn"
He came and took our "sinful" place . . .

Let's appreciate this precious gift
Of His "amazing grace"
Let's not trample it underfoot . . .
And bring disdain and disgrace

But let's live in the power
Of "His Spirit" and His light
Then we can walk in love
And by faith and not by sight . . .

Be a "doer of the Word" . . .
Not letting deception have its way
But walking out His purpose
Every single day . . .

He says, "guard your heart"
Don't let your flesh . . . chart your course
Or you will live in loss
In heartache and remorse . . .

But let your spirit rise and rule
As you walk in God's footprint and His plan
And you will walk right into
Your personal promised land . . .

CHAPTER 60

John 5:14-15

This is the "confidence we have" in approaching God . . . that if we ask "anything according to his will" . . . he hears us . . . and if we know that he hears us . . . whatever we ask . . . "we KNOW" that we "have what we asked of him."

Faith is activated to receive . . . where the will of God is known . . .

This little story shows that everything that happens in our life is "Father filtered" and always with our best interest in mind.

A certain King had a male servant who . . . in all circumstances . . . said to him . . . My king . . . do not be discouraged when things you don't understand happen because everything God does is perfect . . . He makes no mistakes.

One day . . . while they were out hunting a wild animal attacked the king. The servant managed to kill the animal but couldn't prevent his majesty from losing a finger . . . Furious and without showing any gratitude, the King said . . . if God was good and perfect as you say . . . I would not have been attacked and lost my finger.

The servant replied . . . despite this I can only continue to believe and tell you that God is always good and everything He does is perfect . . . He is never wrong . . . Outraged by this response . . . and his loss . . . the King ordered the arrest of his servant.

Even while being taken to prison . . . the King's servant told him again . . . God is good and perfect . . . He makes no mistakes . . .

After a few days the King left alone for another hunt and was captured by savages who use human beings for sacrifice to their gods . . . On the altar . . . the savages checked out the King and found that he did not have one of his fingers in place . . . They took him down from the altar and he was released. He was considered imperfect and not "complete" . . . so he could not be offered to the gods.

On his return to the palace . . . he ordered the release of his servant. When the servant came before him the King said . . . my friend . . . today God was really good to me . . . I was almost killed . . . but for lack of this single finger . . . I was let go.

But now I have another question . . . If God is so good . . . why did He allow me to put you in prison? My king . . . the servant replied . . . if you had not put me in prison . . . I would have gone with you . . . and would have been sacrificed instead of you . . . because I have no missing finger . . . My King . . . Everything God does is perfect, He is never wrong.

So often we complain about our life, and the negative things that happen to us, forgetting that in God . . . everything happens for a purpose . . . He is a God that knows the end from the beginning . . . and all of our life is filtered through the hands of a loving and merciful Father . . .

CHAPTER 61

Filled with His Spirit

So many "traditional" believers have been "vaccinated" with religion and they can't "catch" the real thing!!! Jesus wants a living . . . walking . . . talking . . . "personal relationship" with you and me . . . and the Holy Spirit wants to be with us in all areas and circumstances of our lives . . .

The hour is growing late . . . there is NO time left to wait . . . Jesus is coming back and He is coming soon . . . Open up your heart . . . and prepare Him room . . . Let GO of dead religion and take hold of HIS Spirit and His way . . . .and make a difference in the life of someone else today . . .

The "church" was not meant to be a "bless me" club . . . . But a living and breathing entity . . . where others will "see" Jesus when they look at you and me . . . Living fully by "His Spirit" . . . not by our flesh . . . and our own mind . . . but relying on His guidance . . . and having thoughts of like kind . . .

FULLY born again . . . and filled with the dispensation of His grace . . . not settling for simply being saved . . . but truly reflecting Heaven's face . . . Religion will never save the world . . . Jesus came to prove that this is true . . .

He came and died . . . poured out His life to have relationship with me and you . . . So don't settle for the old . . . step into the new . . .

Rise and shine . . . your light has come . . . He's calling us to ALL His ways . . . to come up to a higher level and a true understanding of His presence . . . TODAY . . . People NEED The Lord . . . and we might be the only Bible that they "see." . . So let's do everything we can . . . so they will see HIM in you and me . . .

What "really" matters is how we represent Jesus and the grace of God!

We are not called to argue about trivial "religious" or "traditional" customs . . . These things only divide us . . . Jesus is our "common denominator" When we lift up HIS name all other "things" . . . our thoughts . . . our desires . . . our wanting our own way . . . they pale and fade away . . . Let's remember that today and every day . . .

His church is not an organization to join . . . it's a "living organism" that we are part of . . . .and the Holy Spirit is our helper . . . comforter . . . Paracletos and friend . . . He is with us from now until the end . . .

God's Word says that the Holy Spirit is "the Spirit of Jesus" (Acts 16:7) and "the Spirit of our God" (1 Corinthians 6:11). He was involved in the creation of the world (Genesis 1:2).

The Holy Spirit caused the Virgin Mary to conceive (Luke 1:35). He guides us into all truth (John 16:13) . . . He convicts us of sin (John 16:8) . . . He performs miracles (Acts 8:39) . . . and intercedes with God for us (Romans 8:26).

He assures us that we belong to God as he "speaks to us deep in our hearts" (Romans 8:16 NLT).

The Holy Spirit is a living gift to all believers and is the divine source of spiritual power and ministry (John 7:37-39; Acts 11:16-17; Romans 5:5).

Mave Moyer

Reverend Mave Moyer is an ordained minister, and she ministers alongside her husband Brother Russ Moyer. They both currently pastor The Revival Centre in Hamilton and Eagles' Nest Fellowship in Copetown, Ontario. They also serve as the apostolic overseers for eight other church plants in Ontario as well as the Eagle Worldwide Retreat and Revival Centre. Mave is the governing official for the Eagle Worldwide Network of Ministries, a spiritual covering for licensed Christian Workers, ministers, churches, missionaries, and para-church organizations.

Pastor Mave is an anointed teacher and preacher in her own right, with a heart to deliver a "Now word" to the Body of Christ. She moves powerfully in the gift of faith, healing, and the prophetic. She is also a gifted singer and poetic psalmist who brings forth "the song of the Lord." She has been involved in producing many country/comedy shows, Christian dinner theatre, and Inner Circle Gospel sings.

She has had the privilege to work and travel with Joan Gieson, a healing evangelist who founded Ministries of Love out of St. Louis, Missouri. Mave attended Rhema Bible Training Centre in Tulsa, Oklahoma.

Russ Moyer

Russ Moyer is presently a missionary / evangelist in Ontario, Canada. He is the founder and president of Eagle Worldwide Ministries. Since his arrival in Canada in October of 2000, he has established the Eagle Traveling Team, which has visited more than 80 churches in North America, Europe, and the Caribbean. He also founded the Eagle Worldwide Retreat and Revival Centre, a beautiful 50+ acre parcel of ground in Copetown, Ontario where annually Summer Camp Tent meetings July through Labour Day along with special conferences and events such as Parade of the Nations, School of the Prophets, and The Elisha Leadership Mentoring Intern Program for youth and young adults.

Russ and his wife Mave have pioneered eight churches in southern Ontario, and are the senior pastors of both The Revival Centre in Hamilton and Eagles' Nest Fellowship in Ancaster. They also provide spiritual covering and apostolic oversight for eight other churches and more than 60 ministers through the Eagle Worldwide Network of Ministries. In May of 2005, John Kelly, C. Peter Wagner and the International Coalition of Apostles commissioned Russ in his apostolic calling and office.

Russ and Mave have a heart to see revival in people groups all over the earth. The Lord continues to open doors for them to minister to indigenous people groups such as the Inuit in the Arctic, the First Nations people in Hawaii, here in Ontario, and in Saskatchewan. In January of 2009 they birthed a First Nations church on the Six Nations Reserve in Ontario. They have also ministered extensively to Africans, Portuguese, French, and the Gypsy Roma peoples.

They are also the founders of Eagle Worldwide Foundation, and The Centre for Excellence, which provides empowerment, educational, and training programs for the underprivileged. This project includes the founding of The King's Way Blessing Centre where they feed and service over 250 clients per day free of charge in the inner city of Hamilton.

Russ and Mave also birthed Spirit Ministries Training Centre, a 2-year practical ministry Bible school.

Russ was a successful businessman for over 21 years and was the recipient of many honors in the business community. He was the founder, president, and CEO of a number of security related businesses, and at one time employed more than two hundred people. He also was the executive producer and host of a weekly, one-hour television program, which dealt with some of the serious issues facing American families, emphasizing Christian values.

In 1997 he traveled to Pensacola, Florida to attend the Brownsville Revival School of Ministry. He graduated in December 1999 and was ordained by Ruth Ward Heflin through Calvary Pentecostal Tabernacle in Ashland, Virginia. Brother Russ is used heavily in the prophetic, deliverance, and healing ministries. He has a heart to see revival in Canada and the nations.

Eagle Worldwide Ministries

Eagle Worldwide Ministries is a prophetic ministry called to bring revival fire to the nations and to challenge, empower and equip the church of Jesus Christ with a powerful message of holiness and hope.

We will focus on the restoration of foundational truths, preparing and equipping the saints for the end-time harvest through teaching, impartation and demonstrations of the gifts of the Holy Spirit.

Eagle Worldwide Ministries includes:

- Six churches in Ontario that were birthed through dreams and revelations and one in Buffalo, NY:
    - The Gathering Place, Aurora, ON
    - Eagle's Nest Fellowship, Copetown, ON
    - Caleb's Place, Orillia, ON
    - The Revival Centre, Hamilton, ON
    - Eagles' Nest Six Nations, Ohsweken, ON
    - His Glory House, Toronto, ON
    - Eagles' Nest Buffalo/Niagara, Elma, NY

- The Retreat and Revival Centre, a place where believers can come and be trained, equipped, and prepared for Christian service.

- Eagle Worldwide Network of Ministries, which is an apostolic and prophetic network that provides spiritual covering, credentialing, and fellowship to churches, ministries, missionaries, Christian businesspeople and government workers that are pursuing their call in church or in the marketplace.

Eagle Worldwide Ministries
Retreat and Revival Centre

Summer Camp Meetings

Come and Get in the Glory!

Second week of July through Labour Day Weekend
Every night at 7:00 p.m.

Every year we hold ten weeks of summer camp at our 50+ acre Retreat Centre. We begin the season with our Parade of Nations, and hold other events and functions, as well as performing water baptisms right in our beautiful lakes!

Spring Camp Meetings

Every year we also host Winter Camp, a 10-day conference in late March with anointed Apostolic and Prophetic ministers. We hold special week-long courses in conjunction with our Bible School, Spirit Ministries Training Centre that can be taken for audit or credit in our Bible School. For more information, visit us at:
www.SpiritMinistries.ca

For more information contact us at:

P.O. Box 39
Copetown, ON, L0R 1J0, CANADA
Tel.: (905) 308-9991 Fax: (905) 308-7798
http://www.EagleWorldwide.com
office@eagleworldwide.com

Eagle Worldwide Network of Ministries

Dr. Russ and Pastor Mave Moyer are the Apostolic overseers of the Eagle Worldwide Network of Ministries, which is a company of apostolic leaders, churches and ministries committed to walk in a covenant relationship with Eagle Worldwide Ministries based on a common vision of a fully functioning New Testament Church.

Our vision is to build a network of churches, ministries and leaders committed to train and release believers in their care into their call and ministry. We believe that all the gifts of the Spirit in the New Testament are for today and that every ministry in the New Testament including prophecy and deliverance is for today. We also believe that there is no junior Holy Spirit and that both youth and children can and should be equipped and released in ministry. We proceed on the basis that the release of the gifts of the Holy Spirit is not to be restricted by age, race, gender or class. This group will come from varied backgrounds including Christian business men and women.

Presently we provide spiritual covering and credentialing for more than one hundred ministers, ministries, and churches in North America.

For more information on our Network of Ministries call us during regular business hours at (905) 308-9991 or email us at: network@eagleworldwide.com.

www.EagleWorldwideNetwork.com